Teaching Primary Drama

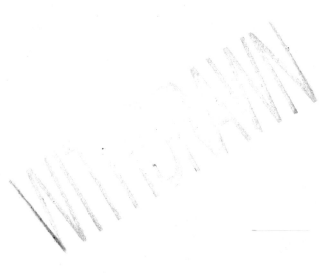

PEARSON

We work with leading authors to develop the
strongest educational materials in education
bringing cutting-edge thinking and best
learning practice to a global market.

Under a range of well-known imprints, including
Longman, we craft high-quality print and electronic
publications which help readers to understand and
apply their content, whether studying or at work.

To find out more about the complete range of our
publishing, please visit us on the World Wide Web at:
www.pearsoned.co.uk.

Teaching
Primary
Drama

Brian Woolland

Longman
is an imprint of

Harlow, England • London • New York • Boston • San Francisco • Toronto • Sydney • Singapore • Hong Kong
Tokyo • Seoul • Taipei • New Delhi • Cape Town • Madrid • Mexico City • Amsterdam • Munich • Paris • Milan

PEARSON EDUCATION LIMITED

Edinburgh Gate
Harlow
Essex CM20 2JE
England

and Associated Companies throughout the world

Visit us on the World Wide Web at:
www.pearsoned.co.uk

First published 2010

ISBN 978-1-4058-9948-2

British Library Cataloguing-in-Publication Data
A catalogue record for this book is available from the British Library

Library of Congress Cataloguing-in-Publication Data
Woolland, Brian, 1949–
    Teaching primary drama / Brian Woolland.
        p. cm.
    Includes bibliographical references and index.
    ISBN 978-1-4058-9948-2 (pbk.)
    1. Drama in education.   2. Drama – Study and teaching (Primary)   I. Title.
    PN3171.W665 2010
    372.66'044—dc22

                                                                2009033196

10 9 8 7 6 5 4 3 2 1
13 12 11 10 09

Typeset in 11.25/14pt Minion by 35
Printed and bound in Great Britain by Henry Ling Ltd, Dorchester, Dorset

The publisher's policy is to use paper manufactured from sustainable forests.

Brief contents

Contents

Preface

A new edition

This book is a new and comprehensively reworked edition of *The Teaching of Drama in the Primary School*. While I hope that most of the strengths of the original book have been retained, this is more than a revised edition. I have consulted widely with practising teachers and lecturers about the changes and have tried to rework the book in a way which reflects the generous observations, recommendations and comments made to me, and which will I hope meet the needs of teachers and students for several years to come. The book has been reorganised and contains several wholly new chapters; those chapters retained from the original edition have all been revised.

Given the substantial amount of new material, something from the original had to go; and I decided to remove chapters about performance. This is not because I have changed my thinking about school plays and performances in primary schools, but because in discussions about these revisions, I realised that including them would have resulted in a book that would have been trying to do too many different things. It may be that the performance material also deserves expanding – but if so, it will be in another book.

Many people commented about the original book that one of its strengths was the way that practical examples were embedded in chapters discussing ideas and approaches. I have retained this feature, adding further examples, and also taking five projects to which brief reference was made in the original and presenting them as expanded case studies in Part 4, 'Extended examples', which also includes two wholly new examples for use with younger children. Where appropriate, I went back into schools and worked on the material with children and teachers. The practical examples and suggestions are all based on extensive work in schools.

When the original edition of this book was published in 1993, schools in England and Wales were in a state of considerable upheaval, the introduction of the National Curriculum in 1989 being just one of many changes taking place within the education system. As the 2009 Cambridge Primary Review recognises, 'Since 1989 . . . (teachers) have struggled to contain a large and expanding national curriculum within a finite school day, week or year . . . .' (Alexander 2009), with the curriculum effectively divided into 'the basics' and the rest. Even teachers who were wholly convinced of the value of drama found it difficult to make time for it in school days which became increasingly prescribed by the rigid frameworks and testing regimes.

In recent years, however, major changes and developments have been taking place at every level in education. The paradigm of a curriculum driven by attainment testing and separated 'basics' is being challenged by pedagogical models which place greater emphasis on creativity, integration and how children learn – with the result that drama, the arts and creativity are likely to be valued more highly in future.

Specific developments, discussed below in greater detail, include:

- *All our Futures: Creativity, culture and education*, the National Advisory Committee's report (DfEE 1999).
- From September 2007 all primary schools in the UK started working to the *Revised Primary Framework for Literacy*, which has given greater emphasis to drama.
- In the National Curriculum for England 2008, the Qualifications and Curriculum Authority published documentation specifically designed to promote creativity in teaching and learning across the curriculum.
- At the time of writing, in early 2009, *The Cambridge Primary Review* has just been published. Whether its recommendations will be accepted by government remains to be seen; but it is quite unequivocal in arguing that the 'case for art, music, drama, history and geography needs to be vigorously reasserted; so too does the case for that reflective and interactive pedagogy on which the advancement of children's understanding in large part depends' (Alexander 2009).

It is in the context of these changes that this book has been reworked.

The aims of the book

1. To champion the importance of drama in the primary school, both as a subject in its own right and as a means of motivating and enhancing learning in other curriculum areas.

2. To suggest a lively and coherent approach to the teaching and use of drama in primary schools.

3. To propose ways in which drama can be integrated with and can complement the demands of the National Curriculum, working within the context of the Primary Framework, taking into account recent developments in Social and Emotional Aspects of Learning (SEAL), PSHE & Citizenship, and reflecting current thinking about the importance of creativity.

4. To offer a wide range of examples of good practice.

5. To suggest ways of planning drama lessons and projects and adapting those presented here.

The book is designed for teachers and prospective teachers in primary and middle schools. The approaches to teaching drama suggested here hold good with whatever age group is being taught. I have, however, included a specific chapter on working with children in the early years to show how many of the ideas described elsewhere in the book (which might otherwise appear either too sophisticated or inaccessible) can be adapted for use with younger children.

I hope it will be of use not only to teachers who have never taught drama and who, perhaps, feel a little anxious about making a start, but also to those with experience and expertise. The book asserts that drama is an important subject in its own right and should be taught as such, while arguing that it has a vitally important part to play in developing the whole school curriculum. It also aims to demonstrate that drama has extraordinary power in motivating children's learning and in developing creativity, social skills and emotional intelligence.

Using the book

The book is organised into five parts. Each of these contains regular cross-referencing, with many of the practical examples revisited and developed from a different perspective in different chapters.

Part 1, 'Drama in practice', looks in detail at the practice and processes of teaching drama. Here, and throughout the book, there are numerous examples given of work in practice. These are all genuine examples of work with children in primary schools in a wide variety of different types of catchment areas throughout the country. The examples are given with the intention of providing a stimulus or a framework, as jumping-off points from which it should be easy to develop your own work. Chapter 4, 'Drama with children in the early years' picks out a number of activities which are particularly useful for teachers of children in

Reception classes and Years 1 and 2. It suggests ways of adapting some of the techniques and strategies suggested elsewhere which might at first seem more appropriate for use with older children.

Part 2, 'Drama in an integrated curriculum', explores ways of using drama at the centre of the curriculum, examining how drama can motivate and provide focus for children's learning in other subject areas. In addition to examining drama and topic work, there are detailed discussions of writing in role, drama and literacy and the importance of exploring *meanings beyond the literal.*

Part 3 focuses on 'Planning and assessment', offering a way of planning drama work which enables you to think ahead while avoiding the problem of making the work overly prescriptive. It contains an account of the planning that might go into an extended drama-based, cross-curricular project and a section on evaluation and assessment in drama – including self-assessment.

Part 4 contains seven 'Extended examples', each of them with its own focus, and each designed for use with different ages throughout the primary range. The examples can be used in their own right – they all contain a range of practical activities – or can be used in conjunction with Chapter 6, 'Planning and assessment'. Five of the seven examples discuss planning considerations and alternative approaches. Each project is prefaced by reference to possible links to the *Primary Framework for Literacy* and/or the *National Curriculum.*

Part 5, 'Resources', includes lists of recommended books, film, television and DVD material, online resources and Internet links. The book ends with a Bibliography and Index.

Drama, the National Curriculum and recent developments in primary education

Teachers who regularly use drama in primary schools do not need specific clauses in curriculum documents or educational reports to convince them of the rich and profound learning opportunities that drama can create, of its great value in delivering other aspects of the curriculum, of the ways it can deepen understanding, develop emotional literacy and engage and raise the self-esteem of even the most disaffected pupils. However, it is worth taking stock and offering a brief overview of some significant recent developments which are changing the emphasis of learning in primary schools.

Even in the years immediately after the introduction of the National Curriculum, when drama was placed within English (which many experienced drama practitioners found limiting), the value of using drama to motivate and enhance work in other curriculum areas was underlined by the curriculum documents for Maths, Science, Technology, History, RE and Geography, all of which referred directly or indirectly to the usefulness of role play or drama.

In 1999 the NACCCE published *All Our Futures.* The report called for 'new priorities in education . . . including a much stronger emphasis on creative and cultural Education'. It asserted that 'Creative and cultural education are not subjects in the curriculum, they are general functions of education.' Of particular relevance to the pedagogy proposed in this book, which stresses the importance of collaborative work, it argues that 'creativity can be expressed in collaborative and collective as well as individual activities' and specifically that drama

> can be a powerful way of promoting skills in reading, writing and in speech. . . . (It) is essentially concerned with exploring social behaviour and the values that underpin it, . . . (enabling) young people (to) investigate a wide range of real and imagined social issues through the safety of assumed roles or situations. This process can generate powerful insights into the values and dynamics of groups and communities.
>
> (NACCCE 1999)

Although there is much in the report that has yet to be implemented, the importance of creativity in education has been recognised by the Qualifications and Curriculum Authority, which has now published documentation specifically designed to promote creativity in teaching and learning across the curriculum. Under the heading 'Why is creativity so important?', the documentation suggests that 'When pupils are thinking and behaving creatively in the classroom, you are likely to see them:

- questioning and challenging;
- making connections and seeing relationships;
- envisaging what might be;
- exploring ideas, keeping options open;
- reflecting critically on ideas, actions and outcomes.'

The *Creativity* documentation recognises, above all, that 'Creative pupils lead richer lives and, in the longer term, make a valuable contribution to society' (QCA 2008, website).

The *Revised Primary Framework for Literacy* (2007, website) also recognises the importance of creativity and acknowledges the importance of the kind of cross-curricular work so central to good drama: 'Making links between curriculum subjects and areas of learning deepens children's understanding by providing opportunities to reinforce and enhance learning.' Drama is recognised in the Primary Framework as essential in the development of literacy, where it has its own strand of learning objectives; but, as demonstrated in the 'Extended examples' in Part 4 of this book, drama also creates rich and powerful learning opportunities in other strands, notably:

- speaking;
- listening and responding;
- group discussion and interaction;
- understanding and interpreting texts;
- engaging with and responding to texts;
- text structure and organisation;
- creating and shaping texts.

Furthermore, drama is an immensely effective resource for personal, social and health education (PSHE) and citizenship. The key here is in the methodology rather than the subject itself. Drama can be taught in a way which privileges children who are good at showing off – which is probably why some adults are anxious and suspicious about the subject – but the methodology I propose in this book attaches great importance to collaborative work, emotional literacy and responsiveness to others. In short, this kind of drama is essentially a collective meaning-making process; collaborative not only between children, but between teacher and children.

Although the *Cambridge Primary Review* has only just been published at the time of writing, and there is no guarantee that it will be implemented, one of its central arguments is that the

> most conspicuous casualties [of a narrowly conceived 'standards' agenda] have been the arts, the humanities and those generic kinds of learning, across the entire curriculum, which require time for thinking, talking, problem-solving and that depth of exploration which engages children and makes their learning meaningful and rewarding.
>
> (Alexander 2009)

Acknowledgements

First, I would like to thank to all those children, students, teachers and colleagues with whom I have worked over many years, and who contributed so much to the development of my own thinking about drama.

Thanks to Catherine Yates at Pearson Longman for commissioning this new edition, and for her advice and support during my work on the book.

In respect of this new edition, I would like to thank all those who have offered feedback and suggestions for revisions, and particularly Liz Taylor, whose advice and suggestions have been invaluable.

And finally, I would like to acknowledge the influence of the late Mary Martyn-Johns, Headteacher of Redlands County Primary School, Reading (where many of the projects described in the book were developed) a wonderful teacher and Head, whose support for drama and enthusiasm for the first edition of this book meant so much.

Brian Woolland

Publisher's acknowledgements

We are grateful to the following for permission to reproduce copyright material:

Figures

Figure 2.1a–e, Figure 3.3a–e, Figures 5.2, 5.3, 5.4 and 5.5: From *The Arrival* (Tan, S. 2006). An Arthur A. Levine book published by Scholastic, Inc. / Scholastic Press. Copyright © 2006 by Shaun Tan. Reprinted by permission of Scholastic, Inc.; Figures 8.1, 8.2, 8.3 and 8.4 from *The Tunnel* (Browne, A., 1989). Illustrations © 1989 by Anthony Browne. Reproduced by permission of Walker Books Ltd, London SE11 5HJ; Figures 9.1, 9.2 and 9.3a–c: From Pieter Bruegel the Elder, *Kinderspiele* (*Children's Games*), Kunsthistorisches Museum, Wien oder KHM, Wien.

Text

Page 22: Poem extract from *Fisherman Chant*, copyright © 1996 by John Agard. Reproduced by kind permission of John Agard, c/o Caroline Sheldon Literary Agency Limited; 189: The poem *Whale* from *Selected Poems*, Secker & Warburg (Thomas, D.M., 1983), copyright © D.M. Thomas, Secker & Warburg, 1983. Reproduced with permission of Johnson & Alcock Ltd.

Every effort has been made to trace the copyright holders and we apologise in advance for any unintentional omissions. We would be pleased to insert the appropriate acknowledgement in any subsequent edition of this publication.

Introduction
'I don't know what it is, but I know it's tickly'

Drama as a subject

Some experienced drama practitioners have suggested that there is a danger in promoting drama as a learning medium, arguing that doing so undervalues it by reducing drama in schools to little more than a service tool. I strongly resist this argument. Drama is an important subject in its own right, but it cannot be taught in a vacuum. As a subject it demands content. The best way to learn about *how* drama works is by using it. Dramatising any subject (whether a traditional story such as *Cinderella*, a moment in history as in The Coming of the Railways or a contemporary social drama such as *The Tunnel*) is a way of exploring the individual's relationship with society. As *All Our Futures* argues,

> Drama is essentially concerned with exploring social behaviour and the values that underpin it. Through improvised drama, and through work on texts young people can investigate a wide range of real and imagined social issues through the safety of assumed roles or situations.
>
> (NACCCE 1999)

In educational contexts drama should be seen as a subject in its own right *at the same time* as being a powerful learning medium. *Dramatic fiction* is the form of fiction with which children are most familiar. Some children may come to school without having ever been read to, but almost all arrive with a wealth of experience of drama on television. We may regret it, but for many children, their vernacular knowledge of drama and dramatic fiction is far greater than of written forms – even if it is largely uncritical. Given that drama, in one form or another, is such an important part of children's lives, it is part of the drama teacher's job to create opportunities which enable them to manipulate the form for themselves, thereby understanding it better.

What do we mean by drama?

So, if we want to teach drama as a subject, if we are to argue for drama to be given its place in the curriculum, it is essential to ask the question, 'What makes drama *uniquely* drama?' If the 'building blocks' of music are Pitch, Melody, Harmony, Tempo, Rhythm and Texture, what are the raw materials of Drama? The following is offered as one possible set of such building blocks:

Role or character

- acting *as if* you were someone else; or
- as if you were yourself in another situation.

Narrative

- ordering a sequence of events or images in such a way that their *order* creates meaning. This is not necessarily the same as storytelling and story plotting, which are examples of the ways in which narrative can be used.

Language

- verbal
- non-verbal (including body language, facial expression, use of space).

There is a danger of over-simplification, but by seeing these as the basic building blocks we get a clearer sense of dramatic activity as a continuum from pre-school play to professional theatrical performance. When a young child says: 'This is my shop', she is pretending to be a shopkeeper, turning a chair upside down to become the counter, making part of the kitchen into a shop and playing with a narrative sequence. The grasp of cause and effect narrative may be only tentative (a young child might well pay the customer for the bag of sugar!), but part of the purpose of the child's dramatic play is to work out possible sequences of events and their consequences. Whether the specific dramatic activity is imaginative pre-school play about shopping, performing at the National Theatre or watching that same performance, the drama is primarily dependent upon all parties agreeing to the pretence. The dramatised, fictional world of make-believe drama draws our attention to aspects of the 'real' world; it helps us to recognise a sense of our own reality, and to understand it better.

Drama is essentially a social art form; it is concerned with how individuals relate to the world they live in; how individuals interact with each other and with society in a wider sense. It therefore becomes the drama teacher's central task to find ways and means by which she can encourage as broad an understanding as possible of these various interactions – between the fictional world of the drama and the actual world; between the personal and the social.

In any dramatic activity there is some shared, tacit understanding of the rules of the make-believe, although there is of course enormous variation in the way these rules are set up. The child playing shops declares the rules simply by saying 'This is my shop . . .'; in the school hall during a drama lesson the teacher might explain 'I shall be playing a part in what we are going to do today . . .'; and in the Globe Theatre, the Battle of Agincourt is represented without a drop of blood being shed. We learn to 'read' the rules, to understand the conventions remarkably quickly.

In educational drama with children we have to consider Role, Narrative and Language; but all of these are dependent on *Context*:

- Where does the action of the drama occur?

- In which historical period?

- What are the relevant social and political conditions?

- What is the setting, the specific *situation* prevailing at the time of the action, the 'back story'?

Context is crucial in understanding the interactions which take place in the imagined world. It may sound absurd to take into account 'social and political conditions' if we're working with young children, but consider the example of a drama with Reception children, in which we're trying to find out if a dragon is friendly. If the drama is going to be successful we will need answers to these questions:

- *When and where.* Does the action take place today, in the here and now, a dragon hiding somewhere in 'Our Town'? Or is our story set long ago with Knights in Camelot?

- *Political and social conditions.* Who makes the decisions? The local Mayor, the townspeople, the children, King Arthur? Who do we go to for help – or who comes to us for help?

- *The back story.* And how did this dragon get here? Has it woken from a long sleep or hatched from an egg discovered in the school pond?

Narrative

The means by which the drama is propelled forward. In a drama lesson the teacher uses various devices to create *dramatic tension* (see Chapter 3), effectively holding the children's attention and interest by ordering events, enactments, meetings, scenes, etc. in such a way that information is withheld or released to tantalise and intrigue as well as to inform. As children learn about drama as a subject, they learn to manipulate dramatic tension for themselves.

The narrative of a drama lesson can function in all the same ways that it can in the theatre; and the range of possible narrative effects is just as diverse. As events are revealed and explored (not necessarily in chronological order – drama lessons frequently have most unusual time structures) so understanding deepens: of the fictional world, of the characters which populate it, of the 'real' world, of ourselves; and of dramatic form itself .

Language

In drama we use a variety of different and varying forms of language – both verbal and non-verbal. Even very young children recognise that different dramatic situations require different modes of speech, different vocal registers – from every day vernacular to something more formal. This playful spoken use of tone, register and vocabulary is a vitally important step in developing literacy, not only in acquiring language, but learning to use it skilfully.

Non-verbal language

In drama, as in our daily lives, we communicate through body language at the same time as we use the spoken word. In addition to the more formal uses of non-verbal language in drama – such as mime, masks, sign language – we also use props and costume (however simple, perhaps a letter and a cloak), sets (a bench, perhaps to stand in for a gangway to a ship setting off for the New World), and perhaps lighting and music. They are all part of what might be defined as non-verbal sign systems; using them effectively is part of the language of drama. In any dramatic activity the spaces in which events take place, the spaces between people and between objects, are themselves significant and meaningful. Any movement-based activity uses space as one of the elements to explore, create and communicate meaning. Simply ordering the space in the school hall during a drama lesson – so that one side of the hall represents the dockside of the Old Country, the other side a ship bound for the New World –

is making the space itself articulate: the space itself made resonant with meaning in a simple but effective way.

Meaning beyond the literal

Even the simplest dramatic activity involves the creation of meaning beyond the literal at some level. The child who turns an upturned chair into a shop counter is using the chair to represent the counter; when the counter becomes significant in the dramatic play it begins to function as a symbol. In drama, props are often invested with symbolic qualities. The particular choice of props helps shapes the contextual world. A large set of keys, for example, might in different contexts signify imprisonment or freedom. No object is symbolic on its own. The context in which it is used gives it its meaning. Symbolic meaning has to be relevant and readable to the group you are working with; the richer the symbolic meanings you create for a group – either as participants or as audience – the richer the dramatic experience. Your job as a drama teacher is to work with the children to tease out these meanings. You do not need to be clever or have a highly analytical mind to do this; what you do need to do is to slow things down and think about them with the children. The questions can be as simple as 'I wonder what it feels like to walk across that gangway and leave a life behind?'

For that, in essence, is what we are doing in drama – collaborating with the children to make meaning.

Making time and space for drama

I've often heard people say they can see the value of drama, but for various reasons they are reluctant to try it for themselves, giving reasons like:

- 'I'm no good at acting.'
- 'I'm not creative.'
- 'The hall's always in use. There's just no space.'
- 'The timetable's so full; and with all the pressures of the National Curriculum, I simply can't find the time . . . .'

Each of these needs addressing.

You don't need to be a good actor

Many of the best drama teachers I have worked with are quietly spoken and would never want to take an acting role in a theatrical production. The issue is dealt with more fully in Chapter 2 in the section on 'Teaching in role'.

You don't need to be creative in an 'arty' sense

As I argue throughout this book, good practice in drama (on the part of both teacher and child) is characterised far more by the ability to listen, to be responsive and to focus attention on the situation than having lots of 'clever' ideas. Put another way, your job as a drama teacher is to focus on problems, rather than presenting solutions.

You don't have to have access to the school hall

What you *do* need is to ensure that there is adequate and appropriate space. Certainly there are times when it is right to work in the hall, but the size, the cold floor, the echo, the noise from an adjacent kitchen, in some schools the use of the hall as a public thoroughfare – all these factors work against you. In many primary schools there are other spaces which are better suited to drama: the TV room, the Library, a music room, an unused classroom. And there are plenty of occasions when the everyday classroom is actually a *better* place in which to do drama than the hall (in which concentration can quickly be lost as children somehow expand to fill the space or become distracted by the PE equipment). This book contains numerous suggestions for such work. If you are going to use the hall, try to make sure you're not going to be interrupted. One of the most misleading notions about drama is that it's always noisy. I've seen a teacher working in the hall and somebody has come in and apologised, saying they didn't know we were there! Quiet, rapt attention is as much a characteristic of good drama practice as invigorating, loud discussion.

You don't need large blocks of time on the timetable put aside especially for drama

While I think that it *is* desirable to have time specifically devoted to drama, it is not essential. Indeed, when you're first starting out with teaching drama it's a good idea not to be committed to a long period in the school hall. This can be nerve-racking and confidence draining. Good drama can take place in five or ten minutes, providing these short sessions are on a regular basis. Infant teachers will be familiar with the idea of focusing and challenging children's play by joining in with it. Older children can equally benefit from the opportunity to work on something for a short period in small groups in the classroom.

Drama is important. It deserves an allocation of time and space which communicates that importance to children and parents; but if you have no previous experience, working for lengthy periods in the school hall is something you can work towards. It is easy to find excuses for not doing drama – working in a primary school is demanding and hectic – but it really *is* worth making time for drama.

At the end of a short series of lessons with a class of five- and six-year-olds I asked them what they thought drama was. One child said acting, another making plays – and then a rather shy child (who had clearly enjoyed our work together without ever pushing herself forward) said, with a beaming smile: 'I don't know what it is, but I know it's tickly.' It may not be a definition, but it's a pretty good description of what it feels like when it's good.

Use of the personal pronoun

I recognise that, although there are many excellent male teachers in primary schools, they are in a minority. Consequently, when writing impersonally about teaching and about drama in schools, I refer throughout to the teacher as 'she'. Many of the practical examples, however, are taken from projects I taught myself; and in those instances I refer to the teacher as 'he'.

1 Drama in practice

This part of the book looks in detail at the practice and processes of teaching drama. It offers a wide range of possible starting points and various suggestions as to how you might develop these – using both small and whole group work. It offers ways of thinking about drama with the intention of enabling you to generate your own material.

The numerous practical examples which you will find in this part of the book are all genuine examples of work with children in primary schools in culturally, socially and geographically diverse social environments.

'Drama with children in the early years' picks out a number of activities which are particularly useful for teachers of children in Reception classes and Years 1 and 2. It suggests ways of adapting some of the techniques and strategies suggested elsewhere which might at first seem more appropriate for use with older children.

Contents

1
Starting points

- Drama and story
- Posters, photographs, paintings, objects and artefacts and poetry as starting points
- Teacher as narrator

Embedded example:

- *Smugglers*

If you have never taught drama before, where do you begin? This chapter suggests ways of getting started, using stories and poems, photographs and pictures to provide a strong stimulus for the teacher and the children. It includes several short examples of work in practice. The practical work and the suggestions given here should be read in conjunction with the next two chapters ('Working methods' and 'Organisation and development'), where many of them are amplified and discussed further.

Extended examples which explore further how you might use known stories, a poem and a painting as starting points for drama can be found in Part 4, where planning for these dramas is also explored in greater depth:

Stories: *Cinderella*

            The Tunnel by Anthony Browne

Poem: Whale Island

Painting: *Children's Games*

A good starting point is one that grabs the attention of the children, intrigues on several different levels, implies dramatic tension and contains the seeds of dramatic possibilities and explorations; so it is important to prepare beginnings and starting points with care; but, if you have had little or no experience of teaching drama, how do you do this? You can use pictures (whether they originate in children's picture books or on the easel of a famous artist), photographs, stories, poems, posters or objects as stimuli for drama.

Chapter 6, 'Planning and assessment', deals with finding ideas for drama as well as structuring lessons and relating drama work to the demands of the curriculum. It is, however, worth bearing in mind that the key to good drama lies not so much in you, the teacher, having good ideas, but rather in working with ideas, finding significance and helping children to examine the consequences of the ideas that they have.

In 1975 the critic Raymond Williams coined the term 'Dramatised Society', referring to the extraordinary wealth of dramatic fictions available to people throughout their lives. It's useful to consider this term, 'dramatic fiction', when thinking about drama in schools; it enables us to see educational drama as part of a broad spectrum of dramatic activity with which you and the children are familiar. Drama lessons need a dramatic structure just as much as plays and films; but you can learn a great deal about dramatic structure by looking at other dramatic forms. A good film, TV play or piece of theatre hooks its audience within moments. If you can do the same in a drama lesson, you will have the children with you and they will want to collaborate with you. In the drama lesson children may not be performing for an audience, but if you can find a starting point or an opening image which intrigues, startles, mystifies and is above all *dramatic*, you are well on your way to a drama session which at least has rich potential.

Drama and story

Many people start teaching drama in the primary school by getting children to take on roles from stories they know and act them out, following the original narrative. This is a safe starting point for the teacher because it gives you the security of the original story; and it can be a pleasurable activity for the children if it brings the story to life for them. The problem of this kind of activity, however, is that it is potentially limiting and restrictive. Although the children may be 'doing' what you tell them to, they are essentially passive. We need to find ways of giving them a personal stake in what they are doing, giving them decisions to make – both individually and collectively – encouraging the class to work *with* you, rather than simply following instructions. You can start to hand over decisions to the children by asking them simple questions about specific actions and moments in the story.

In *Jack and the Beanstalk*, for example, Jack leads his mother's cow to market:

- How does he prepare for this journey to market? What does he need to take with him? Suppose the cow is reluctant to move – how does he persuade her? What might he say to her? How is he to persuade her to go with him? It's not easy leading a cow when it doesn't want to move!

- What kinds of things might the bean-seller say to Jack to persuade him to exchange the cow for beans? *How* might the bean-seller talk?

- *How* does Jack climb the beanstalk? I wonder what it feels like to climb something so tall if you're scared of heights? I wonder what he imagines he might find at the top?

By responding to these simple 'How' questions, the children are beginning to make interpretative decisions and to make the story their own. It's also important to note that addressing the question of 'How' focuses on the *situation*: dwelling on the moment, rather than simply moving quickly from one moment to the next. This is an important principle of drama. How you develop situations in depth is examined in the next chapters.

If you choose to use existing stories as starting points, the work can be much more exciting if the drama develops from the story and beyond it, rather than merely illustrating it. When participants are given responsibility for the action, when they make key decisions and then work through the consequences of those decisions, the opportunities for learning through drama are likely to be far greater than if their actions in the drama are decided for them by an existing narrative. You might find, for example, in your work on *Jack and the Beanstalk*, that the bean-seller is unable to persuade Jack to exchange the cow for 'magic beans' – in which case you might devote time to Jack's attempts to raise money at the market. Thus the *situation* that Jack and his Mum find themselves in is more important than clinging to the known story, and exploring that situation is going to result in work of greater depth than simply enacting in a prescriptive way a series of predetermined moments.

One of the problems of 'acting out' a known story is that the children already know how it ends. Thus they do not feel the dramatic tension of not knowing what will happen next. If the tension of not knowing what happens next is lost, it has to be replaced by some other kind of dramatic tension. When we go to the theatre, we often do know what is going to happen to the characters whose stories we are watching (when we see a production of a Shakespeare play, for example). What keeps our interest then is the exploration of *how* and *why* people get into the situations that they do. Here are some further ways of using a known story to develop dramatic situations with rich potential:

- Stop the reading of the story before the end (as written) and work with the children on the situation at that point in the story, slowly working towards their own ending.

- Explore what happens before the written story starts.

- Explore what happens after it ends.

- Look at what's going on elsewhere while the well-known story is taking place.

- Consider how we can move people from 'offstage' in the story they know to the centre of our drama.

Thus, thinking about the story of *The Pied Piper* in this way might lead you to the following situations, any one of which you might explore in drama:

- The first people who realise that rats are causing serious problems in the town of Hamelin trying to persuade others that that's what the problem is.

- The people of Hamelin trying to find their own ways of dealing with the plague of rats.

- The people of Hamelin trying to find ways to investigate their corrupt town council.

- Persuading the Pied Piper to return our children to us.

- The children, who have been led off and held prisoner by the Piper, planning an escape.

- In a neighbouring town where they hear The Pied Piper of Hamelin story as a rumour: what if this town has its own plague of rats, and they don't know what to do about it? Here, we could use the story directly: perhaps the drama might start with a telling of the rumours that they had heard about events in Hamelin . . . .

Note that each of these examples offers a situation and a focus for action, but *not* a resolution. The dramatic tension arises from *not* knowing – either *what* will happen or *how* we might achieve what we are aiming for.

While still considering using stories, an alternative approach would be to start working on the drama *before* reading the story. You might set up a situation similar to that in a story you want to introduce, but not let the children encounter it until after they have finished their own version of it. This has the added advantage of arousing the children's curiosity in the story when they do encounter it, encouraging them to be active, imaginative, speculative readers. The Giant Awakes, one of the short examples in Chapter 5, is loosely inspired by Roald Dahl's *The BFG* and Ted Hughes's *The Iron Man*, but most of the children who took part in this drama did not know either of these stories when we embarked on our drama. After the drama had finished, the teacher read *The BFG* and *The Iron Man* to the children. They were spellbound; they had a stake in both stories, and were fascinated by the similarities and differences between the drama they had helped create and the published stories. This concept of 'ownership' of material is important in all teaching, but especially in drama. Anyone, child, adolescent or adult, who learns enthusiastically and willingly will learn at a far faster rate and at a more profound level of understanding than if coerced into it. Of course, children should be numerate and literate from an early age, but there is something more important than learning to read, and that is *wanting* to learn to read. Imagine a child going home at the end of school and saying, 'We're reading *The Iron Man*; it's great, it's just like our drama, only in the book he . . . .'

Narrative tension and slowing down the drama

It is worth reiterating a point here which will be picked up again later: the importance of a strong narrative in drama cannot be underestimated – you have to 'hook' the children into the work – but the really valuable learning takes place when you intervene in the action to slow it down, to examine what's going on between people at the moment of high tension, not when the narrative is flowing quickly. Children often want to rush on and find out what happens next. You should use their enthusiasm, but channel it: hang on tightly to the reins and stay where you are and explore that moment in detail. It's been said that drama is simply about people 'in a mess'. This is useful in that it draws attention to the importance of situation, but there has to be potential for resolving the 'mess' if there is to be dramatic tension; and if the possible resolutions create dilemmas, those in turn generate possibilities for negotiation and persuasion. An example from *Jack and the Beanstalk* serves well here: if Jack is emotionally attached to the cow, doesn't want to sell it, then the exchange between him and the bean-seller is going to be far richer than if he simply can't wait to get rid of it.

Posters, photographs, paintings, objects and artefacts, and poetry as starting points

In the introduction I argued that the key building blocks for drama are:

- Role
- Narrative
- Verbal and non-verbal language.

I then went on to develop the need for these to be seen in specific contexts. When we're working from existing stories, some of the building blocks for drama are already present: the story gives us characters and possible situations, and some important questions have already been answered for us:

- Who is involved in this drama?
- What has happened up to now?
- When and where is it taking place?
- What is the problem inherent in the situation that is going to give us a focus for our dramatic exploration?

Using the same method with other stimuli (such as a poster, photograph or a painting), we might expand on those simple questions:

- *Who* is involved in this drama? What are the roles? What groups of people are affected by it?
- What is the *frame* through which we view the story/image, i.e. from whose point of view do we see it? This idea of the *Dramatic Frame* is one which will be expanded upon in detail in Chapter 3.
- *What has happened* immediately prior to the start of the drama? In film and TV scriptwriting terms this is sometimes called the 'back story'. In drama it's often not good to know what happens. That's what we're going to find out in the drama itself.
- What is the key issue? This will help maintain a clear focus.

Using a poster

Figure 1.1 Smuggling poster

Example

Smugglers

Possible roles/groups of people involved

- The smugglers
- Unwilling smugglers
- Family of smugglers
- Crew of a Navy ship
- The people/person who put up the poster
- A community which relies on the smugglers
- A community which is terrorised by the smugglers
- A film/TV crew making a documentary about the smugglers.

Possible frames

- The class are the smugglers confronted with the consequences of their actions. An adventure story.
- We are trying to find out what really happened all those years ago. A cross-curricular historical investigation.
- We see the actions of the smugglers through the eyes of those who have to stay at home and live with the fear of what will happen to them. A family drama.
- The class as people who have lost their livelihood, offered the opportunity to become smugglers. A social drama.
- Navy personnel who have friends and relatives amongst the smugglers. A moral dilemma.

Possible 'back stories'

- 1782. The smugglers have been bringing in contraband for several years. It is a way of life for the community. The Customs and the Navy are beginning to crack down as the loss of income from taxation makes it difficult to finance the Navy against the growing threat of invasion from France.
- This same community has just heard what has happened to a neighbouring village, where relatives have been imprisoned for withholding information about their own family, thought to be smugglers.

- A group of smugglers, who have been involved in this 'trade' for a long time, are on the point of deciding to 'go straight'. But it is difficult. How do they get rid of their smuggled goods without incriminating their families?

- Modern day. A small coastal community – long ago famed as a haunt of smugglers. Everybody in the village has some connection with the smugglers of old. Everybody can tell some story. Maybe they even have things in their attics which will bring back old stories.

The unanswered question or key organising question

- How do people survive when they are outside the law? What sort of pressure does that put on their families?

- How do we deal with the stress that results from family loyalties being in conflict with the law of the land?

- How do people stand up for what they believe is right when they are under enormous economic pressure to do otherwise?

- How does a small self-sufficient and self-contained community deal with an invasion of its privacy?

Possible starting points – using the strategy of teacher in role:

- The poster is pinned up in the Hall when the children come in. Teacher looks carefully at it, then turns to the class, in role, and says: 'We're done for. We're outlaws now. We can't return to our families.'

- The poster shown to the class by the teacher; 'This was nailed to the tree on the village green. I've taken it down. I'll not have anyone inform-ing on my son.'

- 'This poster, which is now kept in the Maritime Museum in Liverpool, used to be displayed on the wall in this Inn. I'm sure that everyone in this village has some story to tell about the events all those years ago . . . .' This could then lead into a whole group drama in which the stories are acted out for a TV crew, or be a stimulus for small group work and/or written work in which the children work alone and in groups to produce the stories and enact them for each other. The *frame* of the investigation gives us a good reason for looking at each other's work and drawing conclusions from it – 'If it's true that some of that treasure is still hidden in that cave, should we go looking for it? What should we do with it if we find it?'

All of the above offer excellent opportunities for cross-curricular work. If the children undertake related historical and geographical research, the drama is likely to be considerably enhanced. Cross-curricular work is discussed in greater detail and with further examples in Chapter 5.

Using a painting

The same sort of questions can be used equally productively with paintings. We can add in the questions:

- In what circumstances might this painting have been made?
- Who painted it?

An extended example, exploring various ways of using Pieter Bruegel's *Children's Games* as a starting point, can be found in Chapter 9.

Using a photograph

You can use a photograph in similar ways to those already discussed. You could also ask the question: Who took the photograph? What was going on outside the frame of the photograph? Why was the photograph taken?

You could create representations of the photograph by making *Still Images* (see Chapter 2), then bring those images to life. You might then consider what the people in the image were doing five minutes/an hour/a week before the photograph was taken, or what they might be doing at various points in the future, thereby creating a storyboard, from which you could then focus on a specific dramatic situation.

Alternatively, you could place the photograph within a broader fictional context. Assuming that the photograph is of a black panther, the teacher, in role as the photographer talking to the class, in role as editorial board, says: 'I've taken this photograph. It's the best I could get.' The drama thus begins in the newspaper editor's office, and immediately encourages the children to start asking questions. Or perhaps, using the same picture, the teacher, this time as picture editor, might say: 'We've been using our own photographers up to now because it's cheaper that way. But we're not getting the results we want. We've heard all these rumours about the panther, but we still don't know whether it really exists. So I'm hiring you as a team of freelancers. I expect the best . . . . Now, what are you going to need to take with you on the expedition?'

In both these examples, the photograph would be 'real', but it is equally possible to use children's own paintings and drawings in this way, giving them the status of photographs within the developing dramatic fiction.

Using objects and artefacts

A few brief examples of the way one might use some carefully chosen (but easily found) objects to provide a powerful stimulus for drama:

A large empty picture frame

With older children, an investigation into the stolen picture. What the picture might have been? Who might have stolen it? Where was it hanging before the picture was removed?

With younger children the same picture frame, concealed beneath a piece of cloth to add to the sense of mystery, could become *A Magic Mirror:* 'I found this in my attic at the weekend. It seems very strange and powerful. I need your help to find out about its powers. Do you want me to take the cloth off it?' We might then walk through the picture frame (the magic mirror) to a magic land, or maybe it could enable us to see things we could not otherwise see . . . . In any event, when working with children, I would start by thinking about the dangers and limitations of the magical powers of the mirror.

An item of clothing

'Can you help me find my little girl. We were at the funfair together and she was wearing this when I last saw her.' This could take us into a drama about the dangers of public places. On the same theme, if the teacher wanted to be a bit more adventurous with it, she could play the lost child: 'Can you help me find my Mum and Dad?'

In the examples given above, the object is used as a starting point in itself. Resources like this can, however, be used at any time in the drama. The quality of the work is always enhanced by good-quality artefacts and visual stimuli.

There are further examples throughout the book which demonstrate the use of resources like those discussed here. See also the discussion of *magic* in Chapter 4.

Using poetry in drama

Thus far we have looked at the way these various stimuli can be used to get started; but the practical examples have all been relatively simple, undeveloped suggestions. Whale Island, one of the 'Extended examples' in Part 4, explores how you might use a poem as a stimulus for drama, develop the drama, and then use the drama in turn to feed back into creative writing work. The example is based on a narrative poem, and follows the principles outlined above, but there are other ways of working with poetry:

- You might ask: Who is writing the poem? Where is s/he? Who is s/he writing for?

- Use the poem as *part* of the drama. Consider, for example, the following extract from the poem *Fisherman Chant* by John Agard:

Sister river
Brother river
Mother river
Father river
O life giver
O life taker
O friend river
What have you
in store
for a poor
fisherman
today?

From *Can I Buy a Slice of the Sky*, John Agard

Consider the following questions: When is the chant used? Who by? Do they speak it aloud? Is it part of a ritual? What might have happened to provoke the line 'O life taker' . . . ?

- You could use the poem to develop movement or mask work, and develop the dramatic situation from that.
- Or use the poem to create sound pictures or choral speaking.
- And we shouldn't forget that poetry grew out of dance and song.

Another way of using poems or stories is to incorporate their language into the role that you take on in the drama. This might be to set a scene, to evoke a sense of place. Thus, you might begin a drama by asking the children to shut their eyes and listen as you read:

Against the stone breakwater
Only an ominous lapping,
While the wind whines overhead,
Coming down from the mountain . . .
We wait, we listen . . .

From *The Storm*, Theodore Roethke

At this point you might ask the children to contribute what they (or we) can hear; you might discuss where they think they are; or you might use this to create atmosphere in the drama about smugglers, for example. Using heightened language in this way adds a sense of weight and importance to the drama; and is likely to result in the children giving more careful consideration to their own use of language.

Teacher as narrator

When you use language in this way, you are effectively taking on a role as a narrator in the drama. At its most basic, this can take the form of the teacher leading the children through a series of activities with them acting out what she says:

> And then they came to a fast flowing river, so they put on their boots . . . and they tried to walk across . . . but it was too deep . . . I wonder how they got across . . .

The problem with this, as noted above, is that it can make the children passive, denying them the responsibility for decision making. If, however, instead of simply prompting them, you use narration as a stimulus, a provocation for *their* ideas, it can be a rich and rewarding strategy, which can also be used to reflect on the significance of the children's work (and the decisions they have made in the drama). It can also move the drama forward, and provide focus and feedback into the developing dramatic fiction. Suppose the class are on an expedition through the rainforest in search of a legendary black panther and plants for medicines. They come to a river. Far better to ask them 'How are we to get across?' than to simply tell them your solution to the problem. Then, having made their way across the river (which might have taken them a couple of weeks of drama time, and, for example, have involved them in negotiations with indigenous people), the teacher might *now* act as a narrator, summarising their actions and giving significance to the work:

> The expedition came to a river, where they found that the equipment they'd brought with them was inadequate. They tried making a bridge out of ropes made from lianas; but they couldn't make it strong enough. They tried to make small boats from fallen trees. But time was running out, their supplies were getting low; they had heard from their guide that the river could soon flood – so two brave girls set out on their own to find the people who lived in this part of the forest, to beg their help . . . .

And at this point, you might draw on some of the children's own writing, and incorporate that into your narrative. Telling the story thus is a way of recapitulating, reminding the children what they have been doing, and what they have achieved, but it is also a way of giving coherence to what can sometimes seem rather entangled.

2
Working methods

This chapter starts by examining *Small Group Work*, then looks in detail at four particular strategies:

- Forum Theatre
- Games and exercises
- Still images
- Teaching in role

For the sake of clarity each of these are dealt with separately. They should, however, be seen as interactive working methods.

The second half of the chapter focuses on *Whole Group Work* arguing that it is a working method which develops out of Small Group Work and gives greater coherence to it.

The chapter concludes with a short *Glossary of drama techniques*.

Embedded examples:

- *Cinderella*
- *The Tunnel*
- *The borrowed bike*
- *The Pied Piper*
- *The Wildman*
- *The Coming of the Railway*
- *Leaving Nazareth*

Small group work

There are frequent occasions in a drama session when children are divided into groups and asked to work on a task. Here are some simple guidelines on the organisation and monitoring of Small Group Work.

The nature of the task

They can be asked to:

- improvise spontaneously – in which, for example, they are given a starting point and asked to develop a scene in role;

- prepare a short play, or scene from a play – during which the children will be working both in role, as the people in the play, and out of role, discussing how they are going to tackle the task;

- create a still image, in which they work out of role to create an image like a statue or three-dimensional photograph;

- do some written work, such as Writing in Role;

- discuss in or out of role – with the results of the discussion to be fed back into the whole group later.

Organisation of the work

In setting up the work you need to pre-plan:

Time limits

How long are the groups going to need for the task? If no time limit is set, the work tends to be unfocused. For many tasks they will need no longer than two or three minutes, and frequently as little as 30 seconds. If, as you're monitoring the work, you think that all the groups are engaged in the tasks and working well, you can give them a little longer. However, it is important not to say they've only got two minutes for something, and then let them go on for ten. Children are good at reading 'hidden' messages – in this case that you don't mean what you say!

If possible, it's a good idea to build a time limit into the dramatic narrative itself – something has to be accomplished before time runs out. This increases the urgency of the task, and raises dramatic tension.

Group size and allocation

It must be appropriate for the task. Do you let children work in 'table' groups, with friends in groups of their own choosing, or do you select the groups? In some classes friendship groups are productive, but there are times when you might want to keep certain children apart because they distract each other, or maybe you want to make sure that boys and girls work together. It is often easier for children if you make the choice on their behalf, and it saves time if they know the groups they are going to work in before they get to the hall or drama space.

One way of allocating groups quickly and randomly, ensuring a good mix, is to ask the children to sit in a circle, allowing them to sit where they want, and then counting round the circle, giving each child a number – one to eight, then starting again. 'All ones here, twos here, threes here, etc.' Thus, with a group of 32 children you'll have eight evenly balanced groups of four.

Setting-up tasks

Pre-requisites for spontaneous improvisation

Clarity is all important. The task should be specific, interesting and within the group's capability. Remember that some children may be anxious about drama; and 'fooling around' is more often symptomatic of misunderstanding and embarrassment than of mischievousness or maliciousness.

Make sure that the context for the drama is clear. When you give out the task, clarify Who? Where? What?

- *Who* is involved in the situation? What roles are they to take on?
- *Where*, and when, is this happening?
- *What* is the situation? What has happened, what is the 'back story'? What's the problem? What's at issue?

The first and the last of these are relatively straightforward but the 'What?' is more complex. It's often better not to pre-plan what's going to happen in a scene, but we do need to know what has happened up to now. It's also import-ant for there to be a problem of some kind, an issue which needs to be resolved, otherwise there's no sense of the outcome mattering.

Choosing an appropriate 'issue', which could range from simple to complex, will depend upon the age, ability and experience of the children:

- 'How do you teach your little sister to tie her shoelaces?'
- 'How will you persuade the Pied Piper to release our children?'

■ 'Can you encourage this reluctant old man to give a radio interview about the way the community used to be sixty years ago?'

Examples

From *Cinderella* (Chapter 7) (Year One. Four per group)

■ *Who?*
All four members of the group are cooks (with older children, they might each have individual responsibilities, e.g. vegetables, meats, cakes . . .)

■ *Where?*
In the castle kitchens

■ *What?*
They have been asked to prepare a banquet for the Prince's Ball. They have to prepare a menu and the food. Issue: Will it be ready in time?

From *The Tunnel* (Chapter 8) (Year Two. Two per group)

■ *Who?*
Brother and sister

■ *Where?*
On waste ground by the tunnel entrance

■ *What?*
Mum has told them that they have to play together, and they'll both be in trouble if they argue. Issue: Can he persuade her to go into the tunnel with him without getting impatient?

The borrowed bike (Year Six. Three per group)

■ *Who?*
Three school friends: A, B and C.

■ *Where?*
After school, in the playground. They have to sort out the problem before the caretaker locks the school gates.

■ *What?*
A has a new bike which s/he thinks has been 'borrowed' by B
B doesn't know anything about the bike
C does know who borrowed it (it is not B), but is frightened of being bullied if s/he says anything about it.

Issue: Can C be persuaded/encouraged to tell the truth.

This *Who / What / Where* information can be conveyed to the children in a number of ways:

- They can all be divided into groups and the whole class can be told 'All A's are . . . ; all B's are . . .' etc.

- Information can be given to each child separately (either verbally or in writing), so that no one knows what information has been given to the others. (This would work well with the *borrowed bike* example above.)

- They can be told some of the prerequisites, and have to work out the others out of role before starting – perhaps they are told who they are and what has happened, and they have to agree where and when the action is taking place.

- Every group can be tackling the same problem, or different groups can be working on different improvisations. In the *Cinderella* example, each group might have a different responsibility in preparing the banquet: one group as pastry cooks, another preparing sauces, while another might be decorators . . . .

- It is also possible to set up the prerequisites through carefully chosen opening lines. For example, 'Mum, can I go out to play?' indicates that the two people in the improvisation are mother and child and that the issue is whether or not the child is allowed out. This could be made much more complex, but there is certainly enough to get started if at least one of the participants has some previous experience. The technique of communicating information through role is an important part of the strategy of teaching-in-role, discussed in detail towards the end of this chapter.

The problems of small group work can be summarised as follows:

- Organisation: the groups themselves need careful organising if the work is to be anything more than structured play.

- It is difficult to work for development and progression in the tasks at a level appropriate to each group.

- Control can be difficult if there is a range of different tasks being undertaken at any one moment.

- It is difficult to offer positive and constructive feedback to groups without ignoring others. Only a limited amount of reflection is possible.

- Competitiveness tends to creep into the work in ways which frequently blind the participants to the real issues being worked on. There is sometimes a tendency for one or two children to dominate the work and this can be destructive and intimidating for others.

■ Audience. It is difficult to share the work without each group showing what they have done – which can be unproductive and time consuming.

These are serious problems, which need to be addressed carefully. We can, however, deal with most of these concerns by giving careful consideration to the ways we monitor and intervene in the children's work, and by addressing key issues surrounding the audience/performer relationship.

Monitoring and intervention – useful strategies

■ Warn the children that you will be going round and 'freezing' work in progress. You then 'spotlight' each group in turn, and the group 'in the spotlight' continues with their spontaneous improvisation from where they are, rather than as a group showing what they have done already. This enables you to comment on the content of what they're doing. With the Castle Banquet, for example, you might say, 'Look at this wonderful cake they're baking over here. I never thought you could get icing in so many different colours . . . .'

■ Instead of performing the whole of their improvisation for the others, one child can report back on what has happened – either in or out of role. This is particularly useful in whole group work – see below.

■ The teacher can enter the small group improvisation in role, using the role to focus and challenge the work.

■ If working in the classroom, rather than the school hall or drama room, the teacher can work with one group at a time, while the rest of the class are engaged in something needing minimal supervision. This allows you to monitor the work carefully and help a group with a task that they might find difficult if unsupervised.

Audience

■ Find a broader fictional context for the creation of the small group scenes, so that the audience are encouraged to comment on the *content*, rather than the lack of specific theatre skills. The overall drama might, for example, be about the making of a television documentary in which people are being canvassed for their opinions about a new relief road. When you look at each of the small group 'scenes' you can accord them much higher status: instead of commenting on the changing position of an imagined door handle, you can discuss which moments from each of the 'interviews' should be kept in the documentary. You thus have an informing context in which to discuss what each of the interviewees said.

■ Develop a sense of the audience having a responsibility, not simply being passive. Still image work is particularly useful for encouraging an audience to become active – see also the discussion of *Forum Theatre* below.

■ Locate the small group scenes in a specific geographic location: a castle, for example, within which each of the groups is involved in different activities – cooking, cleaning armour, building new fortifications, growing food, etc. Now when you 'spotlight' the work, the groups have an interest in other people's work, they want to know what's happening. This is what we should be working towards when work is being shared: creating a desire to see other people's work because it matters within the drama, because everybody's work affects everybody else's in some way.

This strategy of setting up interactive and interdependent small groups is effectively what is happening in *Whole Group Drama*.

Forum Theatre

The origins of *Forum Theatre* are described briefly in the 'Glossary of drama techniques' below. The following is a simplified account of a method of working that has been used and adapted by many drama teachers. In essence Forum Theatre focuses on the work of one small group while activating the whole group; the spectator becomes an active, interventionist participant in the developing drama. Augusto Boal, who originated *Forum Theatre*, coined the useful term 'spectactor' to refer to these participants. Here I use the term 'Forum Theatre' loosely – to indicate a collaborative process in which the whole class are invited to contribute suggestions and offer assistance to a small group participating in a dramatic exchange.

As we have seen, three of the commonest problems associated with Small Group Work can be summarised as follows:

1. Difficulties in providing appropriate and useful feedback to individual groups.

2. Difficulties in showing or sharing the work. How do you ensure that those children who are watching are actively engaged in the 'performance', and not simply whispering about the scene they have prepared?

3. Difficulties experienced by the children in commenting on the work of their · peers in a constructive way.

Forum Theatre avoids all these. At its simplest, two people (or a small group) enact a scene or a drama while the rest of the group watch. The spectators, however, become interactive participants in the drama. This can be done in one of three ways:

1. Spectators can become advisers to one or more of the 'performers'. This advice can range from 'constructing' a character to offering suggestions for dialogue. The 'performers' can similarly ask for help. The teacher can take on a role, but actively involve the whole class in creating and 'performing' the role.

2. Spectators can take over the 'performers' roles.

3. The scene can be replayed in ways suggested by the spectators, as if the spectators not only have access to the rewind button of a video recorder, but can also change what has already been enacted.

The initiative to stop the scene and try it in another way can come from spectators, performers or the teacher. The strategy gives the audience a stake in what is going on.

Example

The Pied Piper

Here is one way that it might work in practice:

Class divided into threes. A, B and C in each group. A's are to play the Pied Piper, B's The Mayor of Hamelin and C's the parent of a child held captive by the Pied Piper. Each group is to try to negotiate for the release of a child. It might help in advance to give certain additional information to each of the three groups independently of the others (see discussion above about *Small Group Work*): perhaps the Pied Piper is prepared to let the children free if s/he can get a good deal; perhaps the Mayor is unwilling to use any public funds to buy off the Piper.

The groups play out their scene for themselves in small groups, but only for a couple of minutes. The teacher should intervene before the children reach their own resolution to the problem.

Volunteers **A**, **B** and **C** (not from the same original group) are then asked to play out the scene centrally. All the other A's (i.e. the Pied Pipers) position themselves behind their 'representative' (with B's and C's similarly arranged). The three now play out the scene.

The teacher stops the scene as soon as it looks as if any of the 'performers' are unable to cope with the situation, and asks their advisers for help: 'What should s/he say now?' 'How might s/he react to that?' Once the children are familiar with this method of working they can manipulate it for themselves – e.g. the performers can ask for advice whenever they need it; the performers can 'Tag' an adviser to take over from them.

Strict parameters and rules do need to be built into the system early on, however, whether it is the children or the teacher who sets them. In particular, consider time limits – both for enacting and for advising, perhaps the performers have to spend at least a minute before they can request advice. One of the great joys of forum theatre is that it is extremely flexible. Once children have seen it at work they often suggest ways of adapting it. Remember that the principle is that the audience is given a stake in what is performed; they are an interactive part of the drama. Here are some further ways in which the method can be used:

1. The teacher, introducing a drama to be based on *The Pied Piper* story, might ask the class *how* they want the Pied Piper to be played. The teacher (in-role) will be the Pied Piper, but s/he wants the class to have a say in the characterisation – so the children 'construct' the character: perhaps –

   Teacher: In the drama I'll play the Pied Piper, but I need your help. I want you to tell me how you want the Pied Piper to be. What does he look like?

   Class: He's rather shifty.

   Teacher: How do you want me to do that?

   Child demonstrates.

   Teacher: What else can you tell me about him?

   Class: He's very clever.

   Teacher: Does that mean he shows people he's clever, or does he keep quiet about it?

   Class: He keeps quiet about it.

   Teacher: So what kinds of things does he say when he first meets the Mayor?

   ▶

2. Suppose this then develops into a whole group drama, with the children playing the townspeople of Hamelin. Instead of having the children go through the small group work suggested above, the teacher remains in role as the Pied Piper and the children are asked to elect two or three representatives who will seek out the Pied Piper and try to bargain with him/her. As they bargain they can now stop the drama and turn (out of role) to their peers and ask for help. The teacher could come out of role, saying 'This doesn't seem to be going very well for you. Would you like to start again and try a different way . . .?'

Children seem to have little difficulty accepting this convention because it is so like the action replays they frequently see on television sports programmes.

Games and exercises

Many teachers begin their drama lessons with a game and then an exercise, arguing that this warms the children up, shifts them from thinking in set ways, encourages them to collaborate, to concentrate, to trust each other. There are others who insist that games and exercises *per se* have no place in the drama lesson, that the best way to learn about drama and to learn how to use it is by doing it. Then, if the drama itself is powerful and effective there is no need to prepare children for it by doing something else. There is, however, a danger of becoming too dogmatic. While games are not of themselves drama, many do contain important dramatic elements: ritual, role play, narrative, symbolic action and symbolic use of space for example. If you want to use a game it's important to give careful consideration to its purpose and/or function.

Advantages of using games

Games can:

- indicate clearly to the children that a different kind of thought process is going to be required of them in the drama session;
- introduce collaborative ways of working;
- focus and channel energies which might otherwise become distracting;
- create useful opportunities for the teacher to assess the mood and interests of the class.

In my own drama teaching I rarely use games with a class that I know well, but when I'm working with a class that I've not met before I often begin the session with a short concentration exercise and then a simple game. Some activities can focus concentration and energy, but I tend to use these activities diagnostically, to give myself time and space to assess the class, to learn about their social health. If they enable me to feel comfortable with the class, then that is important. We need to challenge ourselves, to move ourselves on, but we also need to give ourselves a safe framework in which to do so.

Disadvantages and dangers of using games

- Playing an active game can over-excite children to the point that all they want to do is play the game. Playing the game takes over the drama session and becomes a means for the children (and sometimes the teacher) to avoid the drama.

- There is frequently a hidden agenda in the use of games. If we come up with a different game each time we do drama, what are we teaching the children? Among other things, that it is the teacher who has all the good ideas, thereby making it difficult to hand over responsibility for decision making to the children.

- While some games may be useful, and it may well be that there should be time in school devoted specifically to playing games, games are not of themselves drama, and it is important that children do not get the impression that they are.

Using games productively

If you do want to start your drama sessions with a game, *don't* feel you have to come up with a different one each time. You are not an entertainer at a children's party. If there is a game which you find effective, use it on a regular basis for a short period, perhaps five minutes at the beginning of each session. Whatever games you use, give children the opportunity to get better at them. You don't need a vast repertoire of games in order to be a highly effective drama teacher.

Games don't have to be the starter or warm-up activity. They can play a part in the drama itself. 'Keeper of the Keys' (Chapter 10) can be used as a test of skill, as part of a broader dramatic fiction.

If you are using a game or an exercise at the start of a session, choose something appropriate. If they've had to stay indoors for a wet break they'll want to do something physically active. A game of tag (see below) may well be just the thing; but if they've just come in from the playground, it would be a waste of time.

Ask yourself:

- Do they need warming up? Mentally or physically? The idea of a 'warm-up', as practiced by professional actors is as much to get energised and focused mentally as to limber the body.
- If they are already excited they'll need something calming.
- What sort of activities are they going to be involved in during the session? A lot of verbal discussion? Non-verbal communication? Movement work? Something involving ritual?

Choose a game or exercise which leads into or complements this work.

- Is it appropriate sometimes to finish the drama session with a game or an exercise which calms and focuses?
- It is possible to use a game as a way of demonstrating to children how they can begin to take responsibility for their own learning. How can you give them the opportunity to make alterations to the rules to give them 'ownership' of a game?
- Games can be used productively by thinking about the dramatic elements within them and using the game to lead directly into other work. What are the dramatic elements in the game you are using?

Tag

There are numerous different versions of tag. All of them contain strong elements of role play, narrative and ritual. The following version is useful to give children the opportunity to channel excess energy – everybody is in action for the whole time it is being played.

- A chases B. When B is caught, s/he freezes, eyes closed, counts to 5, then chases A. The game continues for as long as you want – or to a pre-set time limit, or when somebody is caught three times, or . . . .

The game can be developed, rapidly turned into a form of role play – a Hunter and Hunted situation – by asking, 'Who are you?' 'Where are you?' 'Why are you running away?' From there it can become an adventure yarn told in movement, with B miming climbing a cliff face, going through tunnels, crossing rope bridges, etc. A has to follow wherever B goes. This, in turn, might move into Still Image work: 'three still images to encapsulate the key moments in the story you have evolved'.

Blind

Again, there are numerous variations of these blind games / exercises. The following involves everybody at the same time:

- Everybody stands in a circle. One person is directed across the circle. When s/he gets to the other side of the circle s/he is gently redirected across again. This continues until s/he feels confident enough to close his/her eyes. Then a second and third person introduced to the circle. The 'game' is one in which the people on the outside are given responsibility for those on the inside, crossing the circle with their eyes closed. The class is competing with itself.

This can be developed thus – in pairs:

- A leads B to a number of different textures.
- Control your partner without words.
- Control your partner without touch.
- 'Blind' person is a Robot.

The game can quickly become the basis for drama if you develop the elements of role play. Thus, for example: B becomes the blind parent of a sighted child being shown round the classroom or the hall by A, a teacher in that school.

Two concentration exercises

When I introduce myself to a class that I am working with for the first time I frequently begin by asking them to sit close by me on the floor and listen with their eyes shut to the sound of a pair of Indian Bells struck together. They are asked to open their eyes when they think the bells have stopped ringing. This not only gives you an excellent control device ('stop what you're doing when you hear these bells again'), but also creates a useful learning opportunity in its own right: 'Each of you opened your eyes at a different time – which was excellent. In drama you've got to do what you think is right. Don't worry if what you're suggesting is different from other people.'

A colleague, who never uses games as such, takes a rather beautiful candle into the hall when she teaches drama. At the beginning of the session, she lights the candle, the children sit round it in a large circle and she asks them to watch the flame, to concentrate on the flame and nothing else. As a 'warm up' activity there's nothing to beat it!

Still images

The idea of the still image is one which has already been mentioned several times both in this and in the preceding chapter. It's a useful technique – not least because it is so adaptable.

Just as children are familiar with drama itself through the dramatic fictions that they see enacted on television and on film, so too they have encountered the idea of still images in other contexts: their own family snapshots, freeze frame on the video recorder, sculptures, waxworks and comic strips.

As with all techniques it's important to be clear about why one is using it. At its simplest the participants use their own bodies to create a three-dimensional still photograph. It is, however, a technique which can be used in many different ways, for example:

■ as a control device;

■ to make a transition from a visual image into drama;

■ to focus on a particular moment in a drama;

■ to reflect on the significance of a given moment, thereby developing understanding of the depths and layers of meaning any given moment might contain;

■ to open up a situation, to broaden thinking;

■ to shift perspectives;

■ to develop understanding of the significance of eye contact and body language;

■ to select and mark key moment(s) in a narrative, thereby developing understanding of narrative structure;

■ to develop understanding of the articulate use of space;

■ to recap on previous work;

■ to represent photographs taken, so they can be examined within a fictional context;

■ to make it possible to deal with fast moving, or potentially violent, events;

■ to shift the children away from thinking about drama in straightforwardly naturalistic ways and into more stylised modes in which, for example, emotions and ideas are given physical representation.

Still image work has the advantage of being easily repeatable. We are not concerned about spontaneity, but with accuracy and detail. We can return to a particular image at various points in a lesson, noting the way our understanding of a given image changes as we understand more about the broader situation.

Introducing the idea

Because the audience can take such an active part in still image work it is something which can easily be used in the classroom.

- As herself, the teacher creates a still image. Children guess what it is – making a cup of tea, turning on the TV, reading the paper. They then create a still image from their own lives – cleaning teeth in the morning, eating packed lunch, etc.
- Teacher 'moulds' a volunteer to create a still image. The children then do the same with a partner.
- A movement exercise – moving round the room without bumping into one another – and at a given signal everyone freezes. 'It's as if I'd just taken a photograph.' You could even use a digital camera, show them the photo, ask them to recreate that moment.

As with all drama work, it's important to move forward at an appropriate pace, to aim for gradual progression. I'll now examine three different ways of using the technique of still image – to open up a drama, to develop understanding of narrative, to focus and reflect on a particular moment.

To initiate drama

- A photograph (or picture) is given to a group(s). They then take up positions as if they were the people in the photograph. When they are satisfied with what they have produced they are asked to bring the image to life – for a short time, perhaps as little as ten seconds. They might then add a line or two of dialogue to each of the animated images. The Extended Example using Bruegel's painting *Children's Games*, uses this technique.
- You might then take five images from a picture story book that the children do not know, and then ask them to use these images as 'staging points' to develop a drama that links the different pictures. Providing you choose appropriate material, this exercise, a kind of simple storyboarding (described in more detail on pp. 80–1), works well with all age groups. With a young, inexperienced group, you might undertake the exercise as a whole class; with older, more able children they could do it in small groups. With older children you might use pictures from a book such as Shaun Tan's *The Arrival*.

Figure 2.1 Illustrations from *The Arrival* by Shaun Tan

- The class work in small groups to 'mould' each other into still images which will function as waxworks or statues in the drama. The making of the images becomes the first part of the drama, in which (for example) the work is inspected by the teacher in role as new Mayor, who commissions a statue to commemorate the return of the children of Hamelin.

- The teacher will be taking on a role in the drama; the class help to construct the role by using the teacher to create a still image of the role. When they are satisfied with the image they have created they take up their own positions in relation to the image, positions which indicate their own role and attitude.

Example

The Wildman

The Wildman is a retelling of an East Anglian story by Kevin Crossley-Holland. Set during the reign of England's King Henry II, it tells of a merman who is captured, imprisoned and tortured because his difference is so threatening to the fishing community.

The teacher reads the first part of the story to the class: a merman is caught in a fisherman's nets. The class create an image of the merman at the moment he is brought to land, surrounded by humans. The teacher takes on the role of the merman, but asks the children: 'How do you want me to look? How should I express fear? Show me how to do it.' When ready, each child then joins in the still image, remembering their position and expressions so that it can be recreated later. Half the group stay outside the image to examine the other half. This technique, sometimes called *Image Theatre*, is described in more detail in the 'Glossary of drama techniques'. We can then move backwards or forwards in time. What led up to the merman's capture? What do each of you feel about it? What does each of you want to do now?

They might then make images of the community's response to the mer-man. A situation has now been created in which the Key Organising Question is likely to be 'How do we deal with the stranger in our midst?' This could be a powerful starting point for a *Whole Group Drama* (see below).

■ The class make an image of something which is then put into a fictional context as photographic evidence.

Example

The children, in role as time travellers, create still images of incidents they saw on one of their journeys back in time, as if these were holographic, three dimensional pictures. The rest of the class then use these pictures as evidence, discussing the implications of what they are shown in order to plan for their next journey back in time (see Extended Example, *Children's Games*).

To develop understanding of narrative

■ Having been working on a drama spontaneously, the class (either as a whole group, or in small groups) are asked to consider the most important moment in the story so far, and to represent that moment as a still image.

This activity – which develops the ability to analyse, to edit, to condense, to focus and to structure narrative (all important skills in other curriculum areas as well as in drama) – can be taken further by asking children to select three key moments in a story line (either one they have heard or one they have themselves developed through drama). Choosing three images should give them a 'beginning', a 'middle' and an 'end'. Dramatic structure is discussed in more detail on pp. 76–8.

This task of selecting and reflecting on key moments can also be a valuable way of recapping from one session to the next when the drama extends over a long period, as it usually does once it becomes part of a project or topic work. It is more interesting for the children than being asked 'Can you remember what we did least week?', it makes them immediately active and reminds them what they were doing. It can also be informative for the teacher, who can see clearly what the children are finding most engaging about the work.

The examples given above imply fairly naturalistic images or representations. However, you can also ask children to create more expressionist images – which represent ideas, feelings or states of mind.

Example

The children are in role as islanders who have decided to abandon their homes because a volcano is becoming active. You could ask each child to say (or write) what they are feeling as they leave the island, but you might first want to focus on the leave-taking in a more active way. In small groups they might make images to show what it's like to experience conflicting feelings of, for example, sorrow, loss, relief, excitement, hope, expectation.

Focus and reflection

Whatever kind of image the class have created, you now have an opportunity to deepen and clarify their thinking. While one groups holds their image still, the rest of the class briefly become spectators, an audience. The teacher can comment on the image, trying to deepen commitment to the work and draw out the significance of what has been made. At the same time you can take the opportunity to try to build the esteem of those class members who lack confidence and are finding the work slightly embarrassing.

Example

The Coming of the Railway (Chapter 13)

The children have been working in small groups to explore the lives of a small rural town as yet unconnected to the railway. One small group of children have decided to be miners. They have created a still image showing their work down the pit – but one child can't stop giggling. The teacher says: 'I see work which is backbreakingly hard; I see people in very cramped conditions; I see people working together, needing each other. And I see one of these miners managing to stay cheerful in these very tough circumstances.' You, the teacher, are taking the work seriously even if they're struggling with it. In my experience this is one of the quickest and most effective ways of drawing children into the drama; you are helping them to make sense of what they're doing, you're showing them clearly that what they're doing matters.

The teacher can comment on the images, as in this example; but with a large part of the class functioning as an audience there is an opportunity for involving them actively in the process and developing the sense that in educational drama the 'audience' should be active and responsible. The class can be asked to:

- Give the image a title or caption.
- Guess what each person might be thinking? What are their hopes and fears in this situation?
- Guess what each person wants to happen?
- Move around the image and look at it from various points of view. How does this change your impression of what you see?

This not only opens up what is going on, but takes us forward as well. The 'thoughts' the characters in the image are given are those which will lead to action.

- You can put one question to anybody in the image, who has to answer in role – or out of role (but be consistent!).
- Suggest a line of dialogue for each character.
- A spectator group can copy a particular image, and then animate it – with dialogue if appropriate.

Above all else the guiding principle is to tease out the meanings inherent in the images; to ask 'What's important here?'

Teaching in role

Teaching in role is a strategy which a great many teachers have found extremely useful. It is most often used in whole group work, but it is also productive in *Forum Theatre*, particularly if the role you take on functions as an *obstacle* which the class (or representatives of the class) have to deal with through argument, negotiation, persuasion and compromise.

It is also useful on a one to one basis, or with a small group – either in front of the class or discretely. Teaching in role is a *strategy*, a means to an end; it is not an end in itself. The purpose is to offer a way of intervening which challenges and focuses the work, which moves it on, which creates learning opportunities and deepens the understanding of the participants.

Teaching in role requires the teacher to play a role in the drama with the children for a specific purpose. The role itself should provide some focus for the drama. This could be as simple as entering the drama as a messenger and passing on information. If you've never tried the strategy before this is a good way of beginning: the messenger doesn't have to stay in the drama. One reason that many teachers find the idea of teaching in role worrying is that they feel that once they have embarked on a role they will have to stick with it for the rest of the lesson. This is to misunderstand the strategy – which demands that the teacher moves out of role occasionally to reflect on the work. It is also important to recognise that you are taking on a *role, not* giving a performance. What matters is that you adopt a set of attitudes, rather than play a character.

To take the *example* of the messenger, consider this simple sequence:

1. the children are in role as the townspeople of Nazareth; *out of role*, teacher has established with them the nature of their work, their commitment to their land, families and places of work;

2. *in role,* teacher enters as a traveller to tell them that she has come from a neighbouring village, where Roman soldiers are delivering a decree that all will have to pay a new tax; the traveller has to go on her way;

3. *out of role,* teacher asks the children about the traveller – what did she say, what does her message mean for them? They might then be asked to consider their response if the soldiers arrive in Nazareth.

More adventurously, the teacher might choose to play the role of the Roman Centurion who reads out the decree. This is a confrontational role. Always remember, however, that at any time the participants in the drama can come out of role to consider what is happening. Indeed, it is vital that they should do so from time to time. If the confrontation between Nazareth and Rome looks like it's becoming unproductive, the teacher can come out of role and ask the children to reflect on what has been happening – perhaps through discussion, perhaps through a short piece of writing (a diary entry, a letter to a friend, a sketch representing how the townspeople feel about the power relationship, or – shifting the perspective – the report that the Roman has to make to his commanding officer).

Types of role

We can classify roles in terms of their *function* and in terms of their *status*. The messenger role, for example, has the function of bringing information; but that information could be brought by a beggar or a King. When we're using role we need to consider both function *and* status. The following lists are not exhaustive, and many of the categories overlap; they do, however, give an indication of the vast range of possibilities open to you:

Possible functions of a role

- *To seek help and/or advice*: 'I've inherited a circus and I've no idea how to look after the animals. Can you help me?'
- *To seek information*: a traveller looking for a lost companion; a curious stranger.
- *To bring information*, to be a messenger: 'I'm getting a signal through from an alien life form.' 'I've been asked to tell you that we all have to fill in a census return.'
- *To co-ordinate*: an investigator co-organising an enquiry into an air crash.
- *To obstruct* or *challenge*, creating an obstacle which the class has to overcome: the mayor, who doesn't believe that the damage in the town is caused by a giant, insists, 'I need to see some proof.' The Pied Piper, with whom the class has to negotiate for the release of the abducted children.
- *To assist the class with their tasks*: the teacher as the learner, someone taught by the class, an apprentice, a deckhand, a new recruit.
- *To be the Devil's Advocate*: enabling / provoking the class into clarifying their feelings and articulating what they believe to be right: 'I don't see why we should share the proceeds.' 'We should leave the whale alone; that's what we've been told.'

Classifying roles by status

- *High status*: King, Queen, Captain on a ship (or spaceship), leader of the expedition, leader of the village, headteacher, team leader, athletics coach, managing director, etc.
- *Second in command*: The Chief in awe of his Adviser (cf. Whale Island), Monarch's dogsbody, Deputy, go-between: 'I can't do anything about it, but I'll tell her how unhappy you are about it . . . .'.
- *Equal status* (on the same level as the class): one of the team, a member of the gang, villager, crew member.

■ *Low status*: beggar, traveller seeking help, plague victim, shipwrecked sailor, refugee, apprentice.

Any role has both a *function* and a *status*; it is effectively a combination of the above. Some of the combinations seem to go together automatically. An apprentice, for example, is low status, somebody who needs to be taught; but often it is useful to think beyond the obvious. Consider, for example, the different challenges posed to the group by the Devil's Advocate who is high status and one who is low status.

Responses to the status of the role

When planning to use teacher in role consider what *sort* of responses to the role are possible. Put yourself in the position of the children. If you were encountering a tyrannical overlord, what would *you* do? This may not, of course, be what they decide! Ask yourself what are the possible and likely responses?

You should think *why* you're choosing a particular role. Think through the likely *focus* it is going to create in the drama, the problems and dilemmas it is likely to introduce.

High status

The advantage of this type of role is that it's similar to the traditional teacher role; you're retaining control. This can be productive, but the dangers are that it can prevent the children from taking any real responsibility for the drama, and that they take their cue in responding to the role from the way that they respond to you. In an encounter with a high-status role the options are few – they can agree to do as they're told (in which case you, the teacher, end up doing all the decision making) or they can refuse; it's a battle of wits and wills: you remain in control or they overthrow you. That *might* make for excellent drama – but be prepared for it. You will need to signal clearly that they can respond to the high status of the role in a way that is *different* from the way they respond to you. When used in conjunction with the *function* of Devil's Advocate you can push the children to a point where they refuse to take orders; where they have to articulate their opposition to you and *persuade* you that what you are proposing is wrong.

You are, perhaps, the captain of a pirate ship, proposing to take on a cargo of slaves because it's easy money.

Second in command

This is a much more versatile position. You can always defer to the 'off-stage' higher authority (which means you're less likely to have a revolution on your hands!); you can seek assistance; you can still play Devil's Advocate; you can co-ordinate; bring information and, importantly, transfer responsibility to the children. One of the dangers of the position, however, is that it's easy to slip into full authority – which is a 'con' that children can see through all too easily.

Equal status

This enables you to ask open questions of the 'What should we do now?' variety. If the children are unused to the teacher taking on a role, however, they will want to push you into an authority role. Providing you resist, this can in itself provide useful learning opportunities: 'I'm not in charge; I can't make decisions for you.'

A curious traveller or stranger can be of equal status, allowing you to ask particularly useful questions in role: 'How do you organise your meetings? How do you make sure that everyone doesn't speak at the same time?'

Low status

This calls for a good deal of confidence on the part of the teacher, but it can be productive as real responsibility for decision making is transferred to the children. It raises the status, and self-esteem of the children. Although the Devil's Advocate role is traditionally associated with high-status roles, you should remember that someone in a low-status position can still have opinions, can still provoke. I have sometimes taken on a role where I have been injured, a plague victim, and used the role to become Devil's Advocate, suggesting that one of the more aggressive boys in a class 'Finish me off.' Risky, certainly; but it hasn't yet failed to get the class – and the child concerned – to articulate their opposition to the suggestion, arguing that while there's life there's hope!

How to prepare children for working with a teacher in role?

Teachers often have more problems with the concept than children: pre-school children will often play with adults, asking them to assume roles (the shop-keeper, the bus conductor); children who play in this way are used to moving in and out of role, are quite happy for an adult to be *in* their play one moment and themselves the next. Infant teachers who go to the play corner and take part in domestic or shopping activities are already using a form of teacher-in-role.

With older children there can sometimes be difficulties. The easiest way to introduce the strategy is to give a few simple demonstrations:

- Role play the opening moment of a simple scene – e.g. 'Why are you late home? You've not been in trouble with your teacher again?'

- Then ask: 'Who was I pretending to be?'

- Ask for a volunteer to join you. Improvise a short scene with a simple but clear beginning: 'Can I go out to play now, Mum?' Try several short scenes on this one-to-one basis. Then try working with a small group, doing the same thing. From there, it is a comparatively small step for you to take on a role in a piece of Forum Theatre, and then on to working in role with the whole class.

Forum theatre and teaching in role

If you are working in Forum Theatre the class can help in creating the role for you. Ask them, 'How should I play this character? What kinds of thing should I say?' 'Do you want this person to be someone who's helpful or who's going to make life difficult for you?' This is a particularly useful question because it also takes the class towards an understanding that drama is often far more enjoyable if the problems that are raised are not easily solved.

Negotiations with a difficult character (e.g. the Pied Piper holding the town's children in the mountain caverns) are better conducted with the teacher taking on the obstacle role because the teacher can judge just how difficult to make the task, can allow the children (both collectively and individually) success when they need it.

Moving in and out of role

Always make sure the children understand how you are going to signify moving in and out of role. As you, and the children, become increasingly familiar with the strategy you can make the boundaries less clear; but initially clarity is all important.

- You might use a cloak, scarf, cardigan which you put on to signify that you're in role. When you take it off again you're back being the class teacher again.

- What props can you use that help *signify* the role – a brief case? A bunch of keys?

- Another simple, but effective way is to say 'I will be playing a part in this drama unless I'm sitting in this chair. And when I sit here it means two things: firstly that we all stop playing a part at that moment, and secondly that I'd like you all to come over and sit down to discuss what we've been doing.'

Further considerations and suggestions

How much knowledge does the role have? Be careful not to use 'superior' knowledge to intimidate. Releasing knowledge slowly not only enhances the drama, it also increases the likelihood that the children will want to get involved in research.

Use the role to defy expectations. Let them find, for example, that authority has clay feet. Use their expectations and then confound them. If they are familiar with *Jack and the Beanstalk*, and you play the giant, allow him to sound ferocious but, when they meet him, to be a *Wizard of Oz*-like character: nervous, lonely and in need of friends.

Thinking beyond the starting point

Using a role to start a drama can be very powerful, quickly engaging children in the situation by creating highly dramatic moments, but be careful not to choose a role which then limits you. Think ahead. How can the role continue to be used?

Example

Leaving Nazareth

The *initial* function of the role is to pass on information that the Nazarenes will have to leave Nazareth for the Roman census. This can be done by:

- a Roman Centurion giving fearsome orders (high status);
- a town elder passing on information and advising them to do what the Romans say (second in command);
- a weak and infirm townswoman who has heard rumours (low status);
- a traveller who has come from a nearby town, where the Romans have already given out their orders (low to equal status).

Having given the information, where do you go now? Is that all the role is good for? The Roman Centurion can return and enforce the evacuation but cannot open up responses. Each of the other roles are more productive:

- The traveller is a stranger whose curiosity can enrich the sense of community. ▶

- The infirm townswoman will need to be helped on her own journey.
- The town elder can help organise the necessary preparations (or resistance), can ask all manner of questions about families and journeys which will help deepen the commitment to the project.

Whole group work

When I first started teaching drama, the image I had of whole group drama was of a large crowd scene in which everybody was acting as a group. I assumed whole group drama had to be about football hooligans on their way to a match or passengers in an aeroplane about to crash; that there might be shades of difference, but that basically everybody would be doing the same thing at the same time. How wrong could I be?

Whole group drama in fact offers individuals great opportunities for personal decision making; it creates opportunities which exemplify one of drama's essential qualities: that it is a social art form, exploring relationships between individuals and the societies which they inhabit. Whole group drama is best seen as an organisational strategy, whereby all kinds of small group and individual work can take place within a unifying fictional context. Amongst the many benefits of whole group drama, the following are, to me, the most significant:

- The creation of an overarching fictional framework creates a coherent context for a range of work both in drama and in other curriculum areas.
- It provides a focus for small group work.
- It makes it easier for the teacher to monitor work.

Suppose we set up some small group scenes about neighbours arguing, trying to resolve a dispute (it could be open-ended, it could be up to the children to sort out the 'back story' or the teacher could prescribe it – a barking dog in one house and loud music late at night in the other). A problem arises when the groups come to share their work – when for long periods children will be passive.

We could still make our drama about disputes between neighbours, however, and organise it as a whole group drama – simply by setting each of the improvisations in a single street. The drama might be unfocused, but we can now ask each group to look at the others' work as examples of what is going on elsewhere in the street. The advantage of this is that it enables us to start focusing on content. We could make a plan of the street; we could ask each of the groups to find a reason to go to someone else's 'house'; we could perhaps ask other people in the street to try to help resolve some of the disputes other people are having.

Nonetheless, the drama is still not very exciting, and the unfocused nature of the work is likely to continue to create organisational problems. To focus it, we need something dramatic, something which will introduce the potential for change in this situation (and which may destabilise it) or, alternatively something going on in the groups which will have the same effect; we need to focus on an issue.

In this instance, for example:

- The corner shop is to be closed and knocked down to make way for a multi-storey car park.

- The street is preparing their contribution to a town pageant.

- An empty warehouse is to be converted into a leisure centre – the inhabitants of the street are actively involved in the planning.

- People in the street are asked to prepare for an influx of refugees who will be looked after in the local church hall.

- A big hole has suddenly appeared in the street! What are we going to do about it? (This starting point is described in the short example The Crashed Space Ship on pp. 111–12.)

We can introduce this issue in a number of ways (or a combination of them):

- The teacher acts as a narrator, telling the story thus far.

- Information is given in the form of a poster, letters, tape-recorded message (as if over the radio), video tape (TV news), on computer screen.

- The teacher introduces the information in role – as a messenger, as a member of the group, as an outsider, as someone giving orders.

- The teacher (in or out of role) presents the class with an image which intrigues, mystifies, challenges.

Where to start? Slow build-up or in at the deep end?

This unifying issue can be presented at the beginning of the drama or at a later stage, after the children have taken on roles and started on small group work. The advantage of presenting the issue at the start of the drama is that the work is focused from the beginning. The danger of approaching whole group work by letting children first improvise in small groups and then presenting them with an issue which you hope will give them a focus is that they remain more interested in what's going on in their group than in the supposedly unifying issue: 'Why should I be interested in the corner shop being knocked down when I never use it, and anyway we've just been burgled?!'

For the more experienced and confident drama teacher, however, the advantage of starting by allowing them to improvise more freely in small groups is that with careful monitoring you can see what interests them, what they want to explore in their drama. It may well be that several groups have had a burglary – in which case the teacher could use this as the focus: 'How are we going to deal with it? How are we going to stop it happening again?'

Chains of interdependency

So far we've concentrated our attention on this one imaginary street. It exemplifies a group of people who have separate lives, ideas and attitudes, who are united because they are in a common space and (if the drama is working) because they now share a common concern: something has happened which they have to deal with by working together.

In creating whole group dramas, we should be aware of the need to ensure that every child feels they have a stake in what is happening and that they can genuinely influence outcomes. One way of doing this is to establish, within the whole group framework, small groups with common interests, which depend on and affect each other. This means that when they watch another group's work they have an interest in what that group is doing because they are all working within the same fictional context.

In the island community described in the Extended Example Whale Island, these small groups might be:

- Hunters
- Boat builders
- Fishermen and women
- Net makers
- Builders
- Farmers – those who tend crops and animals

- Woodcutters
- Woodworkers – carpenters and carvers.

We can use the technique of spotlighting – focusing attention on one group's work: 'Look what's happening on the farms.' If the crops have been destroyed by the storm or animals have got loose, it will affect every group. As children become more experienced they establish their own interdependent relationships, but initially it requires careful questioning by the teacher: 'You're a woodworker. Who do you get your wood from? How do you help the builders?'

We can use this simple technique to establish the way group members interact amongst themselves and with other groups. This type of work, in which the children are playing at their roles, is frequently a necessary stage in the process of building commitment to the drama; and it is one which adults find just as useful as children do. It can, nevertheless, get out of hand and we should always bear in mind the need to intervene, to challenge, to focus the work, to use this period of 'dramatic play' (or 'busy time' as Dorothy Heathcote has described it) to provide learning opportunities.

One simple way of deepening the 'play' is to ask each group to consider what special skills each individual brings to the group. In the case of the woodcutters, for example, by asking:

- Who knows those parts of the forest where the best trees grow for boat making, for furniture making?
- Who is best at climbing trees?
- Who makes the tools?

It may be time consuming, but what this does is ensure that every child feels they have a special role and that their presence or absence will affect what happens in the drama.

Working in this way, setting up a whole group which functions as a community, frequently leads drama teachers towards work set in villages, small towns or on islands. These self-contained communities cannot easily call upon outside forces to solve their problems; the problems of the drama remain within the group. Good drama is about dealing with the mess we find ourselves in, not calling up some outside agency to solve all our problems. Bearing that in mind, we find ourselves setting whole group dramas on spaceships or sailing ships, in medieval castles, on expeditions; and what all these have in common is that within the setting it is comparatively easy to ensure that each participant has an essential role; we can create clear chains of dependency, thus ensuring not only that each child has a stake in the drama, but also that they have an interest in each other's contributions.

Allocating roles

How can you ensure that every child has a role?

If the dramatic starting point is strong and the situation is clear, children will usually find roles for themselves. There may, however, be occasions when you want to be sure that every child has an appropriate role. This might be because it will give you, the teacher, more confidence in what you're doing, in which case the simplest way is to discuss the likely roles and ask for volunteers before the drama proper begins. This will not, however, solve the problem of certain children taking on what appear to be menial roles. We should never allow the drama to reinforce any child's feeling of poor self-esteem, and this problem needs to be tackled. The simplest way is to ensure that once the drama is under way these roles become highly significant in the drama. For example, the person who offers to be a cleaner on a spaceship (far more often than you might expect) becomes the person whom the alien wishes to communicate with.

A slow, but dramatic and effective way of allocating roles is to come to the children (probably gathered in a circle) and ask them who's who in role: 'I'm a stranger here. Where can I buy bread? And who supplies you with flour? Who works with you?'

Each person goes in turn to one or more other(s) in the circle, saying who they are and what dealings they have with them.

The only problem with this approach is that it can become rather competitive and nerve racking for those children who don't get 'chosen' early on. When I use it I ensure that I have some 'special' roles 'up my sleeve' as it were, so that the children who are approached last are allocated roles which, at least potentially, are the most important.

Alternatives to community-based drama

Basing whole group work on a community is a relatively simple way of organising a drama project. It is, however, by no means the only way of organising whole group work. The class can take on the role of any group of people unified by a common concern or problem, just so long as we ensure that every child has an active role to play. The class can be, for example:

- Detectives investigating a crime: The children might go into the hall and find a frame with the picture cut out of it; an empty cash box; or a desk and chairs overturned, papers strewn all over to give the impression of a ransacked office.

- Archaeologists exploring a Roman settlement, reconstructing events.
- Architects or builders preparing to build a new leisure centre.
- RSPCA officers who have to deal with the animals in a badly run zoo.

In each of the above examples the children have been asked to take on the role of 'people who know'; and it is this which gives them their stake in the drama. The work could be enhanced by the teacher working in role alongside the children; but it is not essential.

Building belief, engagement, commitment

Do we want children to believe in what they're doing? Do we want them to be involved? The word 'belief' is frequently used in connection with drama. I hope that they are engaged in the work and committed to it, but I don't want them to believe it's real; they have to be able to stand apart from the role-playing. It is an important issue, and has led to some serious misunderstandings about the teaching of drama.

It is in periods of reflection that the real learning occurs in drama, when people are given the chance to think about what they have been doing. Children, remarkably, often understand this better than many adults. Even very young children have little difficulty in the notion of moving in and out of role. Frequently in whole group drama we need to stop the drama and move out of role to think about the situation, the decisions that have been made, the actions that have been taken.

The problem with the word *belief* is that it seems to imply a single-mindedness, a deep identification with character which is not only unnecessary, but often counterproductive. It is as if involvement in 'character' is the highest goal. This is no more true of professional actors (who are well aware of the need to stay detached from the roles they play night after night) than it is for children taking part in a drama project, who need to keep their own wits about them, thinking about the meaning and implications of what they say and do and make.

When outsiders watch a drama class they frequently comment on how 'involved' the children seem, noting that they appear so intent on their work that they don't seem to notice onlookers. I think children are in fact often aware of the onlookers, but are making a choice to stay in role; their engagement with the work in hand, with the issues and problems of the drama is more interesting to them than the observers.

So how, in whole group drama, do you build this commitment to the work and engagement in the issues? How do you shift children from glib, superficial, mocking comments (usually symptomatic of nervousness and insecurity) to deeper, considered responses?

There is no single, simple answer. Your own commitment to the work is vitally important. If you take it seriously, the children will follow your lead. Beyond that, a range of strategies are valuable:

- raise the status of the children, make them important in the drama;
- develop the drama beyond single lessons into extended projects;
- use the strategy of teacher-in-role to challenge, to redirect and make sense of glib responses;
- encourage research that supports the project in hand, so that the children see the drama work in a wider context;
- develop inter-curricular work, which itself enhances the drama;
- give careful consideration to your questioning, and create opportunities for the children to formulate questions of their own;
- build in periods of reflection;
- make the work as visual as possible, trying wherever possible to create visual images and symbols rather than simply talking.

Discussions and meetings

One of the criticisms sometimes levelled at the whole group drama approach is that it seems to involve lots of meetings and discussions, and that this dis-advantages those children whose grasp of language is uncertain. Certainly, there is a danger that meetings can turn into heated discussions involving only the teacher and the more articulate members of the class.

Whole group drama, however, is not a *type* of drama, but an organisational strategy; as with any strategy, it can be well used or misused. There are occasions when the strategy demands whole group discussions and it is all too easy to be lulled into thinking the drama is going well simply because one group of articulate children are thoroughly engaged in the work and able to vocalise their ideas, even when another group are left out of the real decision-making processes. There are, nevertheless, ways of ensuring that even the quietest and least articulate children become active participants in meetings and discussions:

- Establish in advance the *purpose* of the meeting – both for yourself and for the children. Is it one at which they will simply be given information by the teacher in role? Or is the intention for the group to reach a key decision? If so, they should know this.

- Establish the *rules* of meetings. Who can speak and when? It is sometimes useful to encourage meetings to be set up as a form of ritual – perhaps people can only address the meeting when they hold a certain talisman (passed from speaker to speaker).

- Wherever possible try to bring in *physical and visual elements* – so that the meeting is about much more than group discussion. When setting it up, for example, ask 'Where do our meetings take place?', so that together you and the children can organise the space in a way which is visually meaningful. Sometimes we'll all be sitting in a circle on the floor – but not always. How do we organise the RSPCA offices or police headquarters?

- If the whole group has to make its decision through verbal discussion it is often better to first present the issue or problem to small groups – then ask each to report back to the whole group. This way everybody has a chance to air their opinions and *everybody's voice is represented* at the meeting.

- *Voting*. Don't assume the children know what is meant by democracy. *Before* putting something to a vote you need to negotiate (usually out of role) what it means. You'll need to get agreement from everyone that, if they end up in the minority, they will abide by the majority decision.

- When you ask for *volunteers*, or opinions, be prepared for the 'Me me me!' syndrome. If we're asking for somebody to persuade the giant to leave us in peace, ask 'What qualities are going to be needed here? What *sort* of person would be best suited?' Somebody who's cunning? Clever? Or perhaps someone who's 'brave'. Then we can explore – through the medium of drama – what those words *mean*. Does being brave mean being strong or overcoming our own fears? Then we can return to the problem of persuading the giant to leave us alone and ask who *in the drama* has those qualities?

- Remember that the essence of drama is acting out 'What if? situations. In any subject we can discuss 'What might happen if . . . ?' In drama we can try things out, we can find out what happens. As a general rule try it, do it and *then* talk about it.

What next? What does a whole group drama look like?

We've had our meeting, we've all got our roles. Now what do we do?

If the dramatic frame is an enquiry or an investigation the children might well be creating still images, which they can then bring back to the whole group. What differentiates this now from uncontextualised still image work is that the audience are now looking at these images in role; they are, for example, interrogating the images as if they were detectives looking at photographic evidence. Prepared small group work can similarly be viewed in context as if it were video material.

There will also be spontaneous small group work, with the teacher maybe intervening in role, or staying out of role, commenting, spotlighting work for others to see. Occasionally the teacher will make use of Forum Theatre techniques; and there will certainly be times when a small group of children will be working in front of the class in a spontaneous improvisation.

There is no set model. The problems within the dramatic fiction are dealt with as they arise; the teacher tries to keep the focus, intervenes as necessary and ensures that there are periods of reflection when everyone can consider carefully the meaning and significance of what has happened. The Extended Example, The Coming of the Railway gives an account of a whole group drama that ran over several weeks.

Whole group drama – some misconceptions and half truths

■ *'It's very demanding in terms of organisational skills.'*
Providing you understand clearly the rationale for whole group work, it is often much less complex than trying to organise a series of unrelated pieces of small group work. The narrative thread creates context which keeps the drama alive.

■ *'It only really works if you are prepared to work in role alongside the children.'*
Working in role definitely helps; it's an economical and effective strategy. But it is not an essential part of the process. If you do choose to use teacher-in-role, there are going to be many occasions when you'll have to step out of role to reflect on the work. You certainly *don't* need to be a good actor to work effectively in role.

■ *'Whole group work and small group work indicate fundamentally different approaches to the teaching of drama.'*
It is difficult to imagine whole group work which doesn't also involve small group work at some point – but with the advantage that whole group work gives small groups focus, purpose and context for their work.

■ *'Whole group work involves endless meetings and discussions and is therefore intimidating to children whose grasp of language is uncertain.'*
As discussed above, be wary of this. Also remember that it is the decision making that is important, not the meetings. Discussions and meetings have their place; but make sure that every child contributes to the decision-making process at some point.

■ *'In order to run a whole group drama effectively you have to be not only very experienced, but also highly charismatic.'*

Many of the best drama teachers I've seen working are quiet and self-effacing. And I have seen relatively inexperienced young students running very successful whole group drama sessions.

To summarise

When you're using whole group drama:

- You must give the class a clear focus to the work.
- Dramatic play, or 'busy time' is an important stage which children need to go through to build up their commitment to the work, but don't expect learning to take place without teacher intervention.
- Periods of reflection must be structured into the process.
- All the strategies and techniques referred to elsewhere in this book (such as Forum Theatre, still image, small group drama) can be used within the context of a whole group drama.
- If the class is working in small groups as part of the whole group, try to ensure that they can see how their work relates to that of others.
- Make sure that every child feels they have an essential role in the drama. This does not necessarily mean playing a big 'character'; but every child must have opportunities to make decisions and influence outcomes.
- Establish that once an idea has been accepted it is not to be denied.
- Negotiate with the group to agree on decision-making procedures; don't assume they understand the workings of democracy!
- When involved in discussions and meetings consider the needs of the children who are less articulate.

A glossary of drama techniques

The following is a short glossary, summarising some of the techniques that can be used in drama. I refer to them as 'techniques' and not 'strategies' or 'conventions', as they are sometimes described in other books. They are tools that enable you to explore situations in depth, ensuring that as many children as possible have a stake in the drama, and that everyone's voice is heard. It is important, however, not to let these techniques take over and become the raison d'être of the drama. All of the techniques described serve to *slow down the drama*, enabling you to encourage reflection, to focus on detail, to tease out meaning. That is what matters.

Conscience alley

Someone facing a dilemma in a drama walks slowly between two lines formed by the rest of the group. As they pass each person, those on one side comment aloud in support of a course of action, while those on the other side give reasons against it. At the end of the alley, the character has to make a decision on the basis of what they have heard. The technique is similar to Forum Theatre in that it gives every member of the group a chance to participate, to allow their voice to be heard. As with all these techniques, it is easily adapted – for example, those on one side of the 'alley' might voice hopes, while the other side voice fears.

Forum Theatre

Augusto Boal, who originated forum theatre, was himself inspired by the work of the educationalist, Paulo Freire. Forum Theatre has been much adapted by drama teachers. At its simplest, a dramatic exchange (involving a small number of people) is played out in front of the whole group. The group, whom Boal referred to as 'spectactors', has the power to stop the drama and suggest alternative directions which it might take, or volunteer to take over a role for a re-run of the action. In this book I use the idea of the forum loosely, as a kind of market place, where ideas are exchanged. Constructing the teacher in role as a character in a drama thus becomes a kind of Forum Theatre.

Image Theatre

This is another technique developed by Augusto Boal, and is described in detail in his book *Games for Actors and Non-Actors*. Essentially it involves a small group making a still image or sequence of images. As soon as the group have been given the title, they try to make the image – but without any talking among themselves – within a given short time limit. When the time limit is up they have to freeze whether they feel they have achieved the task or not. One person then steps outside the image, looks at it carefully and models all the participants as if they were clay or plasticine. When satisfied, s/he steps back into the image. Then the next person steps out and does the same. Each person can change the image as much or as little as they like – but they must not return the image to the way it has been before. When every person in the group is satisfied with the image, it is compete. The exercise encourages non-verbal communication and co-operation. See Boal 1992: 164–5.

Mantle of the Expert

Mantle of the Expert is an approach to teaching and learning initially devised by Dorothy Heathcote in the 1980s. She has continually developed the approach ever since; and it has been taken up and used in many schools by numerous practitioners. Heathcote's work was inspirational in the development of educational drama, and is often associated with Mantle of the Expert. The central idea is that participants take on the collective role of 'experts' in a drama, or 'enterprise', as Heathcote now terms it. They might be anthropologists investigating the disappearance of a small island culture, curators in an art gallery researching a painting by Bruegel, or naturalists charged with the task of releasing caged animals back into the wild. They are being asked to agree, for the duration of the project, to imagine themselves as that group of anthropologists, curators or naturalists, with appropriate jobs and responsibilities. The approach expects all participants (children and teachers) to take their responsibilities seriously. We cannot magically 'endow' children with expertise. What we can do is to give them responsibilities within the drama, interact with them as if they had that expertise, listen to them, be advised by them, and crucially allow them time to build up their own sense of responsibility within the world of the project.

Further information about Dorothy Heathcote's work and Mantle of the Expert can be found in 'Online resources and Internet links' in Part 5, 'Resources'.

Role on the wall

This provides a visual aid for developing thinking about character(s), a means of recording information about characters in graphic form. The technique is used, and described in greater detail, in the Extended Example, *Cinderella*, pp. 147–58.

Still images / freeze frame

Groups or individuals use their bodies to create a three-dimensional image of a given moment, as if that moment had been freeze-framed on a video or DVD. This can be used to focus on body language and facial expressions; as a way of moving from comic strip or storyboard images to improvisations. It is also useful in conjunction with *thought tracking*.

Thought tracking

Pupils, other than those playing a role, are given an opportunity to speak what they think the thoughts and/or feelings of characters in role might be. This can be added to still images / freeze frames or become part of a Forum Theatre – for example, 'What might she be thinking at this point?' Conscience alley is one way of formalising thought tracking.

Twilighting

It is sometimes useful to move into a drama gradually, to prepare the ground, to spend some time in a kind of twilight zone between reality and the drama. An example can be found at the beginning of The Coming of the Railway.

3
Organisation and development

This chapter starts by looking at the issue of control and discipline, and the related skills of questioning and reflection. This discussion then moves on to examine specific ways of developing, deepening and enhancing the work, looking in particular at narrative and non-verbal language.

- Control and discipline
- Reflection
- Questioning skills
- The key organising question
- Narrative: structure and dramatic tension
- Narrative: storyboarding and sequencing
- The dramatic frame

Embedded examples:

- *Reflection and writing in role*
- *Reflection through discussion*
- *Lost treasure*
- *Smugglers*

Control and discipline

As in any teaching, two of the most important requirements for good control are careful organisation and clarity. The teacher does not need to know exactly what will happen in a drama and cannot usefully plan a story line very far ahead, but you should give careful thought to the organisation of the lesson. This demands that you answer the following questions:

- How will groups be divided?

- How will the situation of the drama be introduced?

- Are suitable writing materials easily available if the children are likely to need these for reflective work?

- What other resources are needed? For example, objects, posters, costumes or materials, data projector.

- How will the space in the classroom/hall be used?

- What register(s) of language do you intend to use?

The children must be quite clear from the outset about the task in hand. What is going to be expected from them during the course of the lesson? We all mess about when we think that what we have been asked to do is silly or pointless. Build into the drama periods of reflection; they give significance to the drama itself and to individual contributions. Above all, remember that if each child feels s/he has a clear responsibility within the drama, control problems are far less likely to arise.

Ground rules

Always establish clear ground rules at the beginning of each session. Keep the rules clear, simple and to the point. If possible try to frame them in a dramatic way – because this is a further pointer for the children showing *how* you are going to work together. It is productive to *agree* these rules with children rather than dictate them. Explain that in the drama lesson you are going to be working *together*, that you will need their help, that you cannot create the drama on your own. This raises their status, makes them important. Drama should be a collaborative process – within agreed parameters – and that in itself helps establish good control and good drama.

Your ground rules might include: how we make sure we can hear each other; who talks and when; how we organise meetings; if the children are working in the school hall, when they can use mats, benches, chairs; whether they're ever allowed to use PE equipment.

Stopping work

You should definitely agree specific ground rules about stopping work. You should make quite clear what signals you will use to indicate that you want them to stop what they're doing. Remember, however, that if you're asking them to become engaged in a problem in any depth, simply clapping your hands and asking them to stop what they're doing can be quite destructive. You need at least two different signals:

1. One which indicates 'stop at once' (something's going wrong and you need to draw everyone's attention to it).
2. One which effectively says 'stop what you're doing and come over here when your concentration is wavering'.

The signal for 1. could be clapping your hands or banging a drum or tambourine. I prefer to use a set of Indian bells – very small cymbals which produce a quiet but high pitched and very pure note which can be heard above all sorts of other noise.

For 2. simply sitting in a chair and saying, 'When you notice that I'm sitting here it means I want you to stop what you're doing and come round.' This may sound rather feeble, but it is very effective. The hidden message to the children is that you value their engagement in their work. Another way is to raise your hand, and for each child to raise theirs and stop what they're doing when they notice. This respects their engagement, while being more obvious and therefore quicker.

Having established the ground rules, explain to the children *how* you will be working – e.g. if you are going to play a role yourself, tell the children that's what you're going to do, and explain what signals you are going to give to indicate that you are going to move into role.

The child's point of view

If you encounter control problems, try to see the problem from the child's point of view. *Why* is the child playing up, misbehaving or distracting others? Here are some common reasons:

■ *Are they themselves distracted?*
   It is not easy for children to concentrate on sharing out the last of their emergency rations if the dinner ladies are putting out tables for lunch. Make

sure there are as few interruptions to the work as possible. Drama makes challenging demands on participants. Interruptions are distracting and embarrassing. I once worked with a teacher who was called out six times in an hour to deal with problems (all of them trivial compared with slaying the Minotaur!). The hidden agenda in such a situation surely appears to the children that 'our drama is the least important thing in the school'. Maybe the children could make a notice to hang on the hall doors – STRICTLY NO ADMITTANCE EXCEPT TO REGISTERED STARSHIP PERSONNEL (adapted as appropriate, and put up with staff agreement). In some schools, where the hall is an architectural thoroughfare, this is far more difficult – but it should still be possible to raise the issue in a staff meeting, and negotiate an agreement that anyone who has to pass through the hall while drama is being taught must be quiet and unobtrusive.

- *Do the children properly understand what is required?*
  Think how you would feel if you were asked: 'I'd like you to be slaves in the hold of a sailing ship.' What would you do? What could you do (other than sit and do nothing, or perhaps be revolting) if you'd been given no further guidance? Suppose, however, the children have to secretly *plan* an escape which the crew of the ship are to know nothing about . . . .

- *Are they embarrassed by the situation or task in hand?*
  This may come from the content of the drama or from its organisation. While it is productive to ask boys and girls to work in small groups together, they find it embarrassing to be asked to choose a partner of the opposite gender for themselves. Don't let organisational oversight get in the way of the work.

- *Do they want to be the centre of attention?*
  There are some occasions when it is educationally valuable to offer such a child the 'centre-stage' for a while through the drama itself. The class may learn a great deal about tolerance from such a strategy. There will be other times when it may be necessary to ask: 'Do you want to take part in this drama, or not? Are you behaving like that to make people laugh or because it is what you honestly believe to be right.' In most cases asking a child to sit out for a while is sufficient 'discipline' providing the drama is interesting enough to draw them back in.

- *Are they bored?*
  Is the task in hand too easily achieved or is pitched at an inappropriate level?

- *Are they unable to tackle the problem?*
  Is it beyond their intellectual grasp? Have you couched the problem in language that is too complex for the child?

- *Are they unwilling to tackle the problem?*
  Maybe it opens emotional wounds. Any teacher is constantly having to make difficult value judgements. Here the key issue is the extent to which the child is likely to benefit by tackling the problem through drama.

If, after taking all this into account, the drama lesson begins to go wrong, it is often a good idea to ask the children to help in analysing why. If this means stopping the lesson, so be it. Do something else. Try not to feel too bound by the timetable. As you gain in confidence you and the children will probably soon find that there is never enough time to do all the things you want to do.

Reflection

It is vitally important to create periods of reflection within a drama when the participants can consider what they have achieved as individuals and as a group; when they think about the significance of their work and examine the implications of any decisions they may have taken. Reflection is one of the keys to good control and organisation in the drama session; it is largely through reflection that children learn to value what they are doing.

Reflection can take place in or out of role; during the drama lesson (as and when important moments arise); at the end of the lesson; in the classroom; immediately before the lesson.

Ideally reflection will:

- raise the status of the children's contributions;
- draw significance from the work and offer broader contexts for what they have achieved;
- help the children understand the meanings and values in their work, and how they have used dramatic forms to create those meanings;
- move the drama forward – both in terms of the narrative and the quality of learning.

Reflection is often thought of as a backward-looking process. There is certainly value in this, but if the reflection also contains the seeds of future action then it is even more useful. The reflective process often involves work in other curriculum areas, be it discussion, IT, writing, artwork; and frequently draws on their own research. The most useful activities are those which stimulate children into thinking dynamically and constructively about what they have been doing.

Example

Reflection and writing in role

Consider the following:

- a painting of a giant;
- a sailor's personal log;
- a letter to a friend left behind after a move.

Each of these could be used to reflect on what has occurred in the drama. But the reflection is likely to be more interesting and more challenging if the activity looks *forward* as well as over the shoulder, as it were:

1. The painting of the giant could become a picture which is going to be used to show a sceptical researcher (the teacher in role?) how big the giant really is – necessarily demanding that the child thinks about the concept of scale.

2. The sailor's personal log might not only record what has happened on the journey so far, but might also speculate about what the crew should do with the merman they've caught in their nets; it might contain thoughts about food and the way it is stored on board ship; it might suggest new ways of storing food.

3. The letter to a friend left behind after a move could contain thoughts about the way the family have been treated by immigration officials, recounting memories, but also hinting at the dreams and fears, the expectations and terrors of what lies ahead.

Discussion

The most obvious way for the teacher to initiate reflection with the whole class is to discuss the work. Such discussion should include thoughts about the *form* of the drama and its *content*. If the children are going to develop skills in drama, time must be given to consider the way language and space have been used:

Examples

Reflection through discussion

- The teacher has been playing the Pied Piper, the children a group from Hamelin negotiating for the release of the children. Out of role, teacher asks, 'How would you describe the way the Pied Piper spoke to you? Where was he looking? Did that make it easy for you to talk to him? I wonder how he would have responded if you hadn't been so angry/polite/upset by the loss of your children?'

Wondering is a very useful skill in drama, and one which we'll return to later, when thinking about *Questioning*.

- The teacher, in role as a Roman Centurion, arrives in Nazareth to give the decree that everybody has to return to 'their own city'; the children as the citizens of Nazareth. The teacher steps out of role and leads the following dialogue:

Teacher: What is your private reaction to that? What are you thinking that you would not want anyone else in the town to hear?

Whatever the response, the teacher can add a further reflection, which could support or challenge the pupil, and in some cases move the drama on.

Pupil: I'm glad he wants us to move. Nazareth gets very dull.

Teacher: Nazareth is a small town, isn't it. And going back to somewhere you have not been since you were a baby could be very exciting. I wonder what you expect to find when you get there?

or

Pupil: I don't want to leave; my son died a year ago. I want to be able to go to his grave on the day of his death.

Teacher: And it's important to mark those anniversaries. I can see the journey may well be difficult for you. I wonder how the rest of us could help this woman?

It is in the nature of the work that we often ask children to make tough decisions in drama. If the class are finding the process difficult it is worth acknowledging and reflecting publicly on that: 'I can't imagine anyone would find a decision like this easy.' Sometimes you need to support the child who appears to be being facetious: 'People often laugh when things are really difficult.' Alternatively, you might comment, 'Making the decision does *seem* to be easy sometimes. We could just toss a coin. It's living with the consequences that's difficult . . . .'

The teacher can help the children reflect by focusing the discussion or task in hand, or can create opportunities for the children to consider their work for themselves. Sometimes we need to reflect publicly, sometimes to provide space for a few moments of private reflection. This might mean the children sit quietly alone while the teacher asks questions which they respond to in their thoughts (as at the end of the Extended Example, *Whale Island*), or the reflection might take the form of a diary, or perhaps an 'emotional map' charting the highs and lows of a journey, an adventure or an exploration.

Showing or sharing work always contains possibilities for reflection. If a small group has shown its work, try to encourage discussion in terms of *meaning*, rather than by judging it. If, for example, a shy child has been very quiet in what is supposed to be a television interview, a positive way of dealing with it is to acknowledge it as something that has happened within the dramatic fiction: 'Most of us would get nervous being interviewed for TV; I know I would. What can the TV crew do to make the situation less frightening?' Much better than booming out in an intimidating voice 'We can't hear you!'

Still image

At the end of a drama session you might ask the children to consider the most important moments in the drama and create (say) three images or 'photographs' of those moments. The activity itself encourages reflection; the children are thinking back over what has happened and making important decisions in selecting the key moments.

If the drama continues from week to week it might be a good idea to adopt a similar strategy at the beginning of each session – a more active way of recapping 'the story so far' than through general discussion. Still image also allows you to slow the drama down and think about a situation from another's point of view. Look at the image which another group has created: what is each person thinking? And what might be the implications of those thoughts?

Children often play in role. A key difference between this type of play and educational drama is that the latter is specifically structured so as to create learning opportunities. Much of the learning that takes place in drama does so in periods of reflection when we are given time to consider our actions. That is why it is inadequate to describe drama as 'learning through action' – which is also why finding time for reflection is vital to good control. The quality of the reflection is necessarily dependent on the questioning skills of the teacher.

Questioning skills

By now it should be evident that it is more important for the drama teacher to develop sensitive and perceptive questioning skills than to have an armoury of clever ideas. It is the children's ideas we should be interested in, not our own. A skilful teacher uses questioning:

- to focus the drama;
- to introduce decision-making processes;
- to encourage reflection;
- to enable feelings and thoughts to be articulated;
- to challenge stereotypes and preconceptions;
- to develop skills of analysis and interpretation;
- to draw ideas from the class;
- to provoke and encourage children in their use of language;
- to draw reticent children into the drama;
- to consolidate learning;
- to build tension;
- to encourage research.

A well-constructed drama session will also create opportunities for children to develop their own questioning skills.

The key organising question

Arthur Miller, the famous playwright, once responded to someone who asked him about the message of one of his plays that when he wanted to send messages he did so by telegram. If he were writing today, he'd no doubt have sent the message 'by text' rather than by telegram, but the point is that it is far more useful to think about plays in terms of the questions they ask us than the things they tell us. *Macbeth*, for example, asks us some very difficult questions about, amongst other things, the relationship between power and sexuality, acquiescence in the face of evil and turning a blind eye to things we would rather not know about. Different interpreters see these questions differently, which is why there can be so many different productions of the same play. However, by formulating the central questions, a director will make the production coherent and give it focus. Exactly the same is true of educational drama. Good theatre asks difficult questions; so too should our drama work. When a playwright embarks on a new play, the starting point is frequently 'What if?' It's the questions that matter, not the answers.

The concept of the 'Key Organising Question' is helpful both at the planning stage and during the project itself. It allows you flexibility whilst giving the work a strong sense of purpose and direction. Here are some examples of Key Organising Questions:

- How can we persuade the Giant to leave us in peace? ('The Giant Awakes', Chapter 5)

- How do we cope when personal loyalties come into conflict with group loyalties?

- How can we deal with bullying without resorting to violence ourselves?

Sometimes (as in the first example) we need to ask the question directly. There will be times (as in the second example) when it's more useful to keep the question at the back of your mind; asking it directly might be too intimidating.

Types of questions

There are many ways of categorising questions. As with most things in drama, there are many questions which slip between and overlap categories, but the attempt to define types of questions is useful if it helps us see more clearly what we are doing and what we could be doing. In the examples given, where a title is given in brackets after the question, that refers to one of the Extended Examples in Part 4.

Open and closed questions

This is perhaps the simplest classification, but beware the simplistic notion that links open with good and closed with bad. Closed questions are sometimes perceived to be those which can only elicit a 'Yes' or 'No' response. The received wisdom is that they are not very productive in drama, where we are trying to open up possible responses. There are, however, times when closed questions are very useful. What is crucially important is that you, the teacher, should be aware of the type of question you're asking. The real problems come when you think you're asking an open question which is in fact closed; and, worse, when you think you're asking an open question which is actually a 'Guess what's in teacher's head question?'

Branching questions

'Do we accept the coming of the railway, or do we resist?' is an example of a closed question. Eventually the railway is either built or it's not. Such questions are particularly useful when the social health of the group is poor; when the group is unused to being given responsibility; when you want to draw specific individuals into the decision-making process, perhaps because they're shy or nervous. An open question, such as 'How should we deal with this man who's come to do a survey for the railway company?' can be intimidating. You need to build up to such genuinely open questions ('The Coming of the Railway').

The better the social health of the group, the more open our questions can be. In the meantime, closed questions can start us on the path to fuller negotiation. When children have seen that their decisions, however small, affect the course of the drama their self-esteem rises enormously.

There are children so painfully shy that they find it difficult to voice publicly 'Yes' or 'No'. If you ask such a child 'How should we respond to the aliens' request for help?' s/he's not likely to respond very articulately. Narrow the possible terms of response by a branching question: 'I understand just how difficult this decision is, but you're the bio-chemist; I don't think anyone else can make the decision. Should we allow the alien to come on board the ship?' The child is going to feel pressured, certainly, but it's my experience that after the decision has been made (maybe simply a nod or shake of the head) the child seems to grow almost visibly. Their decision has been crucial.

Questions that seek clarification

In many school situations teachers use questioning to check up on how much children have taken in. In drama there is rarely a single right answer, and it's often more appropriate to phrase questions so that it is the teacher who does not know, the children who do the clarification:

- 'Am I right in thinking that . . . ?'
- 'Now, can I get this clear in my head . . . ?'

Questions that simultaneously convey information and demand a response

Consider what information each of the following questions feeds into the drama:

- 'What time did we agree to meet again?' (*The Tunnel*)
- 'Where can we find a map of the caves?'
- 'What makes this particular tree so special?'
- 'With the situation so dangerous, why did you leave the children playing in the square?' (*Children's Games*)

Questions that suggest implications

Don't ask open questions to which you don't want open responses! If you ask 'What should we do now that there's a reward been offered for our arrest?' you should be prepared to accept the response: 'Find whoever put up the poster and kill them.' You may ask further questions which suggest implications, but if you don't want to deal with the implications you shouldn't have asked the question in the first place.

Consider the implications of:

- 'Do we really want to know who put up the poster?'
- 'What's on your mind as we think about who might do the killing, then?'
- 'And will that put an end to the offer of a reward?'

Questions that build tension

- 'Can I trust all of you to keep this secret?'
- 'Is this bridge still strong enough to carry us all?'
- 'What will happen if we fail?'
- 'Just how dangerous is this Giant?'

These not only build tension, but also imply information, in that they raise the possibility of things going wrong.

Questions which seek information and/or stimulate research

Consider the wide variety of research opportunities (in role and out of role) which are created by the following:

- 'What kind of food should we prepare for the banquet?' (*Cinderella*)
- 'What do we have in our homes today that you think people didn't have a hundred and fifty years ago?' ('The Coming of the Railway')
- 'How many people use the corner shop regularly?'
- 'I wonder what really caused the plague of rats?'
- 'What equipment should we take with us on our expedition?'

Questions which encourage deductive reasoning

Consider what children might actually be required to do in response to each of the following:

■ 'Why do you think the Giant has come to our town?'

■ 'What evidence do we have that the Alien means us no harm?'

■ 'What makes you think that the smugglers were never caught?'

■ 'What gives you the feeling that we'll be safe here?'

Questions which lead to decision making

Sometimes these are closed, branching questions (as above):

■ 'Should we leave the spaceship unguarded?'

Sometimes they are much more open:

■ 'What should we do about . . . ?'

Remember that questions that are *too* open, such as 'Well, what do we do now?' make considerable demands on the group socially as well as dramatically.

General skills related to questioning

■ Be prepared to wait. If there is a silence don't jump in. Give the children time, a chance to respond.

■ When you ask the whole group questions, give careful thought in advance to how you are going to deal with a flurry of waving hands and shouted answers.

■ Allow and encourage your own curiosity as well as the children's. Develop the skill of wondering, of asking 'What if?'

Developing questioning skills in children

There are particular roles that children can play which themselves encourage the use of questions:

■ The detective

■ The investigator

■ The reporter (TV, radio, newspaper)

■ The interviewer

■ The researcher.

Use the strategy of teacher in role to create a character who is mysterious or enigmatic; then give groups the opportunity to question the role to find out more. In small groups they can decide in advance on the questions they want to ask. It's often productive to limit the number of questions allowed to each group. This encourages them to listen to other people's responses.

When sharing still image or small group work, instead of asking for comments about what's been seen, ask them to formulate questions about it. This can be a useful strategy in developing performance drama. The questions which are asked about a still image tell us a great deal about the narrative interest in that image. For example, an image is presented of one child threatening another. A comment about this might be, 'It's about bullying.' The responses to 'What questions do you want to ask here?' might range from 'What happens next?' through 'What has he done to deserve this?' and 'What can he do about it?' to 'They're both looking in this direction. What have they seen?'

Narrative: structure and dramatic tension

Throughout this chapter I have argued that the most productive way of maintaining good control is through the content of the drama itself. As in all teaching, if you can 'hook' the children, interesting them in the subject matter, you are less likely to encounter disruptive behaviour. In drama we have a great advantage over other subjects in that we can use the power of narrative to intrigue and draw children into the work at the same time as teaching them about narrative; teaching them how to manipulate it for themselves.

Ask a class to shut their eyes, play them a recording of footsteps and ask then what they have heard. Some children might say 'the sound of footsteps', but others will begin constructing a story – a prisoner being taken to his cell, perhaps, Mum or Dad coming upstairs to say goodnight or a murderer walking along the landing. As human beings, we tend to want things explained, and stories (for the most part) create meanings for us. Play another sound effect – perhaps a door opening, keys jangling, a car moving off, a bomb exploding, or a dog barking – and it becomes difficult not to link the two sounds together and make them part of the same story. However little 'plot' there might be in some of our dramas, there is always narrative of some kind; a series of events or incidents in which the sequence itself is meaningful. We should *use* narrative and dramatic tension to structure our work in such a way that it draws the children in, but we should also be sure that we are teaching *about* narrative.

At whatever level we are working (be it with children in their first years in school, or with adults) the first engagement with the work comes through dramatic tension of some kind. The teacher should plan carefully – first to create dramatic tension, and then to use it productively.

Let us first examine how we can generate and use dramatic tension, and then look at how we might teach narrative.

At its most basic level dramatic tension originates in the questions the participants are being encouraged to ask themselves:

- What's going on here?
- What's going to happen?
- We know something's going to happen, but *when*?
- How did things get to be like this?

We can create dramatic tension by building up expectations. For example, islanders hear on the 'radio' (a pre-recorded message on audio recorder?) that a hurricane is heading their way. They know it is coming, but they don't know when. Or, working out of role, the teacher can simply say, 'Something big is going to happen in the drama, I promise you, but I'm not going to tell you what it is until it happens.'

Tension is also created when we expect one thing, and something else, quite different occurs. Here, as elsewhere, we can learn by watching the way tension is raised in theatre, TV drama and films.

Dramatic tension, and indeed drama itself is frequently associated with confrontation; but it is not confrontation itself which creates the tension in dramatic terms. It creates the *possibility* of dramatic tension. The argument between two children which runs:

Tom: You stole my packet of crisps.

Jane: No I didn't.

Tom: Yes you did.

Jane: No I didn't

is certainly confrontational but is of little interest dramatically. It becomes interesting when one of them stops for a moment and thinks; and the other looks worried, and suddenly we start to wonder 'What's going on here? What's this about?' And we don't know what's going to happen next. It is *not* knowing which makes it dramatic. Confrontation only creates the possibility for drama when it raises the possibility of *change*. It is change, or at least the *potential* for change, which underpins any consideration of dramatic structure.

In most dramas we start (however briefly) with a *stable* situation:

- the prisoners of war in the prison camp;
- the smugglers who regularly bring their booty ashore;
- the islanders whose way of life has been unchallenged;
- the giant who has been buried under the ground for hundreds of years;
- the children who go to and from school every day.

That stable situation is then made unstable:

- somebody proposes a breakout;
- the smugglers hear of a large reward for their capture;
- a terrible storm comes to the island and a whale beaches on the shore;
- the giant awakes;
- the children discover a great hole in the ground.

The instability of this new situation has to be acknowledged and built on. In other dramatic forms this is the job of the writer, director and actors. In educational drama it is up to the teacher to create and build the tension in collaboration with the children. To do so we make use of theatrical structures, which are built on contrasts; the contrasts between:

- light and darkness;
- sound and silence;
- movement and stillness.

In this way we ensure that the pace of the drama lesson doesn't remain constant. There will be times when things are happening quickly, and times when everyone is hushed and expectant and everything hinges on a symbolic gesture. Thus we create suspense, mystery, an air of intrigue. Using the power of secrecy and confidentiality, we take children into our confidence.

This does require, however, always being alert to the dramatic possibilities. Where confrontations occur that are likely to create possibilities for change in the dramatic situation, you should welcome them. These are the moments that of themselves create difficult dilemmas; the stuff of good drama. In short, *don't avoid the drama*! Seek it out. A well-taught drama lesson creates a social environment in which it is safe for children to make 'bad' decisions and explore the consequences of these decisions because they are working beneath the protective shield of the role and within the protective framework of the dramatic fiction. Indeed, there are times when 'bad' decisions create the most powerful learning opportunities and the most exciting drama.

Example

Lost treasure

'Bad' decisions and good drama – working through consequences

A Year 6 class is working on a drama about undersea exploration. They are seeking the wreck of a Roman Galley off the coast of Italy. (Some useful Geography and History work in this.)

They prepare for their expedition, making lists of equipment and supplies, passports, negotiating to hire an appropriate boat (Maths as well – they have to calculate the costs involved – and Science). When they get to Italy, the teacher decides it's all getting a bit cosy: there's a lot of good work going on in other curriculum areas, and the children are enjoying it, but where's the drama? There's been nothing very dramatic since the secretive and highly confidential opening, when the teacher started with, 'I've been told about the wreck of a Roman Galley, which is buried in mud off the coast near Pompeii; and it's said that when it sank it was carrying great chests of treasure from Egypt.' So the teacher decides to present a challenge. Taking on the role of an Italian Customs Officer, she comes on board ship and tells the children that the authorities know about their activities. The crew will be able to keep half of all the treasure they find, but it will all have to be declared.

After the official has left, the teacher comes out of role and asks the children what they are going to do. What if they say 'We'll kill the Customs Officer'? Superficially, it would seem that the teacher's job is to steer the children away from such an action, but to do that closes off some valuable learning opportunities. Killing the Customs Officer is morally wrong, of course. But if we deny that as a possible choice to the children, we withhold from them a dramatic experience which, if handled carefully, will create situations which enable them to explore the morality of the situation. Allowing them to make the 'bad' decision does *not* sanction it – far from it. But it is essential to follow up the decision and pursue the consequences rigorously.

▶

They decide to kill the Customs Officer. So we make plans, and seizing the opportunity offered by what was initially a rather glib suggestion results in something highly dramatic and profoundly challenging. The killing is difficult and unglamorous. Within the fiction of the drama they have to confront the isolation that comes from being outside the protection of the law; they are asked to change roles, to be a colleague of the officer informing her husband and family what has happened.

Similar situations occur in 'Whale Island' and 'The Deserter' (documented in Part 4) where specific techniques for exploring the consequences are examined in greater detail.

Narrative: storyboarding and sequencing

At its simplest, a narrative is a sequence of events. When we change the order in which things happen, it changes the meaning of the story. This apparently simple concept of cause and effect is at the root of much of our early work on narrative in drama. In drama children make decisions, and then they see the consequences of those decisions. This is another good reason for not pre-planning the outcome of decisions in drama; why it is good to work on the 'back story' but not to pre-empt the outcome. If we set up tasks which ask children to plan what happens at the end of their plays, we not only eradicate the tension, but also lose considerable learning opportunities. Whole group drama, in which you use reflective moments to consider not only the content but the form of the drama itself, provides one of the most effective ways of learning about narrative. There are some specific exercises you can undertake which draw attention to the narrative and structural elements of the work, and enable children to transfer many of the skills they learn through drama into literacy.

One of the most effective of these exercises is the use of storyboarding, which in effect is telling a story in pictures, much as in a comic strip. The concept is borrowed from film makers who always translate a written script into a visual storyboard before embarking on filming. Many theatre designers, and some directors, do the same thing in the preliminary stages of working on a design. Children are familiar with the idea through comic strips. You don't need to be a good artist for the exercise to be highly effective; and it's a useful link with Media Studies.

- Choose the five or six key moments in the drama. Make them as still images. Draw these images in comic strip style.

The exercise is about selecting the key moments and expressing these visually. The diagrams of the story of the *Pied Piper of Hamelin* (see Figure 3.1, pp. 82–3 and Figure 3.2, pp. 84–5) illustrate how a story can be told through storyboard – and also how the same story changes when told from different points of view – in this example from the Piper's and from a Hamelin family's.

The choice of five images in each of these storyboards is deliberate and significant. In developing a sense of dramatic structure it is useful to think in terms of an odd number of scenes. Three images give a clear sense of a beginning, a middle and an end. This can then be developed into five scenes or images. If the first frame is the beginning of the particular narrative, and the third is the middle, the second connects the two; similarly, the fourth, the middle and the end. In this way a short scene can be developed not only into a longer scene, but also into a sequence of scenes. The key is always to break work down into manageable tasks.

You might then ask the children (working individually, in small groups, or in collaboration with you as a whole group – depending on their experience and ability) to add captions to each frame in the storyboard. This summary of the narrative offers a means of further reflecting on a narrative. Adding dialogue in comic strip boxes can provide a strong visual means of recording a basic script. The exercise of storyboarding is also useful at a more sophisticated level, when working with older groups as a means of seeking out the structure of a scene, whether the group is realising an existing text or devising the scene. Creating a storyboard focuses on a key aspect of narrative: the way that sequencing produces meaning. If you change the order in which events occur, you also change the relationship between them, and with it our understanding of how and why things happened they way they did.

This is an exercise which could be used in conjunction with image-sequencing exercises you might do in Media Studies.

Look at Figure 3.3 on page 86, which shows images from *The Arrival*, and using the blank storyboard below it (Figure 3.4), put them into a sequence which tells a story.

The dramatic frame

When considering the narrative structure of our drama lessons we are essentially thinking about a sequencing of events. As we are doing this we should also consider the point of view from which those events are seen – as shown in the storyboards for *The Pied Piper*, which follow.

Figure 3.1 *Pied Piper* story from the Piper's point of view

Figure 3.1 *continued*

In real life we see the world through our own eyes. Much though we might sometimes like it to be otherwise, events do unfold as they happen. Moments which we would like to savour disappear in a flash and moments which embarrass us seem interminable; but drama is not real life. One of the things we are trying to do as we explore situations is to deliberately slow down time, in order to tease out meanings and implications and explore situations in depth.

- In drama we act as if we were someone else, or as if we were ourselves in *another* situation. In other words, we see the world through another's eyes.

- In drama we can slow down time, we can stop and examine a particular moment, we can go backwards in time. If we are in a drama which moves forward at 'life speed', it is because we have chosen to do so.

Figure 3.2 *Pied Piper* story from the family's point of view

Figure 3.2 *continued*

These things are just as true of educational drama as they are of traditional theatre forms.

It is this manipulation of time and viewpoint which enables us to choose an appropriate *frame* through which to explore our dramatic situations. Thus we can examine any given sequence of events dramatically by seeing these events through different eyes and from a wide range of different perspectives. We can thus look at the same events from close up, as if we were part of them, or from a distance by framing our drama as an investigation or an enquiry.

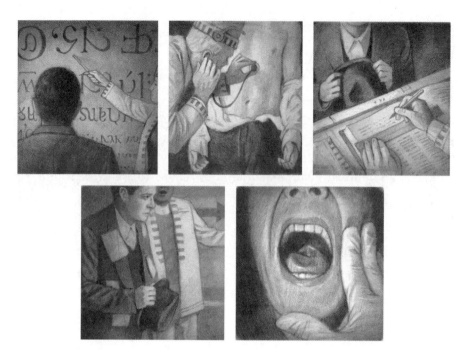

Figure 3.3 Five illustrations from *The Arrival*, out of sequence.

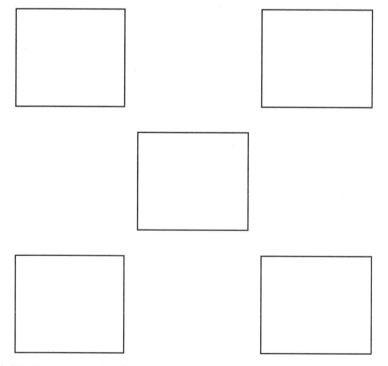

Figure 3.4 Blank storyboard: using the images from Figure 3.3, put them in a sequence that tells a story.

Smugglers

Let's return to the *Smugglers* example discussed in the 'Starting points' chapter. Several examples of possible frames were suggested there. Here are some further examples. There is nothing absolute about the headings suggested. The court, the enquiry and the investigation are in many ways similar, and all will include elements of reconstruction. The intention in suggesting them is to stimulate further thought about other possible frames.

The adventure story

- *Time – 1782*
  We are smugglers. One of us (the teacher in role?) has seen the Reward Poster . . . .

- *Time – 1782*
  We are townspeople, knowing that smugglers use caves in the nearby cliffs. We want to stop the smuggling and claim the reward, but one of us (teacher?) is worried . . . .

- *Time – the present day*
  The teacher needs the children's help to find the smugglers' treasure, which is rumoured to be hidden in a cave that is difficult to reach. If we find the treasure, what is it? What should we do with it? To whom does it rightfully belong?

- *Time – the present day*
  We are a group of divers undertaking an exploration of the Cornish coast, trying to find the wreck of the ship pictured in the Smuggling poster. What equipment do we need?

The reconstruction

- *Time – the present day*
  The events of 1782 are reconstructed (and acted out in small groups) from letters, maps, pictures, posters, historical documents. This could be for a television documentary about the town or for a town pageant.

▶

The investigation or enquiry

- *Time – 1797* (five years after the poster is displayed)
  Three Customs and Excise Officers have 'disappeared'; we are trying to find out what has happened to them.

The court

- *Time – 1792* (ten years after the poster was first published)
  Several villagers are in court, accused of aiding and abetting the smugglers. Is there a difference between the evidence given in court and what really happened?

Dramatic frames for *The Pied Piper*

What was life in Hamelin like before the rat plague? Now that in itself is not really dramatic; there is no dramatic tension in the situation – but there could be if we placed it within the frame of an investigation set after the disappearance of the Pied Piper and the children. How did we allow ourselves to be taken in by that man? The frame gives us a reason for looking closely at apparently normal events.

- trying to discover where the Pied Piper came from;
- investigating how the Mayor of Hamelin became the Mayor.

Drama teachers have as much to learn from playwrights and screenwriters as they do from other drama teachers. Think of popular films like *ET*, *Ghostbusters*, *Close Encounters of the Third Kind*, *The Sixth Sense* or *The Others*. There had been numerous movies about ghosts and aliens before these. *One* of the many things which made these films successful was the particular dramatic *frame* they used.

Chapters 5 and 6 give further suggestions about finding an appropriate frame.

4
Drama with children in the early years

- Play
- Making a start
- Intervening in the children's own dramatic play and structuring play-corner activities
- Whole group work
- Organisation
- Pretend and reality
- Magic
- Still image and Forum Theatre with young children

Embedded examples:

- *The Magician who Lost his Magic*
- *The Circus*
- *The giant's toothache*

Many of the examples of practical work given elsewhere in the book are also specifically intended for use with children in Key Stage 1, and several of the drama projects documented there are accounts of work with children in their first years at school – notably 'The Crashed Space Ship' and 'The Giant Awakes' in Chapter 5; and the Extended Examples *Cinderella* and *The Tunnel*.

Play

From a very early age we use various forms of play to make sense of the world. Although there are a number of different theories about play, there is certainly a consensus about its importance in human development. As Richard Courtney argued, '. . . drama is inextricably linked with the origins of society itself . . . . In one sense, the origins of society are the origins of drama because it is by impersonation and identification that man, in all history, has related himself to others' (Courtney 1968). Young children play with language, trying out sounds before they start experimenting with words. Children's own free play is not in itself drama, although it is a close relation. They use role, they develop stories, they give symbolic significance to the spaces in which they play – a bed becoming a pirate ship, the arm of an armchair becoming the back of a horse. They use this role play to explore their interests and their concerns in similar ways and for similar purposes to the way we use drama – to explore and develop their understanding of the world.

Drama with children in the early years – what's the difference?

Drama with children in their first years of school differs from drama with older children only in content and organisation, not in basic approaches to the subject. Much of the theory and practice suggested elsewhere in the book holds good when working with very young children, although the methods by which you undertake the work will be different, and you will need the focus of your work to be clear.

In fact, what young children demand of us is not that we dilute the work, but that we make it more exciting, more tightly focused. With older children we can sometimes talk our way out of a sloppy beginning, whereas with young children we have to grab their interest from the outset.

Five, six and seven year olds are perfectly capable of working on drama for an hour and a half or more at a time, but they need clear tasks, strong images and narratives which are intriguing and above all dramatic. Script writers are often urged to 'Take your characters closer to the centre of the action.' This is also useful advice for drama teachers – especially when working with young children. If, in your drama, a giant has come to town, you can have your council meeting to discuss what the townspeople should do about it, but what the children really want to do is to meet the giant!

Working with this age group, organisationally we can go in several directions:

1. We can lead them through highly prescriptive sessions in which they act out the teacher's scenario.

2. We can provide a small group with a stimulus in the play area and let them get on with their own play, occasionally intervening (as described below).

3. We can participate (both in and out of role) in their small group work.

4. We can work together as a whole group in which there is a clear focus and a clear task.

There are times when each of these strategies is appropriate, although I am reluctant to use the first unless it serves a clear purpose. When I do use it, it tends to be as a way into a narrative for which the children themselves will take increasing responsibility. 'The Giant Awakes' (Chapter 5) is a good example of a highly prescriptive opening which is then used to stimulate more open-ended work. There is also some merit in using a prescribed scenario to gradually open up decision making to the children as, for example, described in the references to *Jack and the Beanstalk* in Chapter 1 and the Extended Example of *Cinderella*.

Making a start

Whatever the age group we're working with (be it five year olds or fifty year olds) the basic elements of drama remain the same:

- narrative;
- role play;
- non-verbal sign systems (gesture, body language, facial expression, the space between people).

All of these are going to draw on the vast range of vernacular knowledge of dramatic fictions that children bring to school with them when they first arrive. Their knowledge and experience of drama will be far more wide-ranging than is sometimes acknowledged. Most of them will have experience of:

- their own play (which is likely to have involved role play – though this is certainly not always the case);
- stories – telling and being told;
- film and television.

Additionally, some of them may well have experience of puppets, pantomimes, and theatres. In some of these the child is an active participant, is making drama of a kind, in others s/he is responding to dramatic fictions that others have made.

All the basic elements of drama are present to an extent in children's own play. However, while many children enter the school having already enjoyed many hours of 'pretend' play, there will be some whose experience of such play is limited and who find it difficult to differentiate between being in and out of role. We need to take account of this range of experience when we plan drama with young children. We can, however, be reasonably certain that they will have at least some common experiences of television dramas; these can themselves provide us with useful starting points.

While an experienced teacher might start by working with the whole class, drawing the shyer children into the drama through the excitement of the drama itself, there is much to be said for working in the classroom with small groups. The best practice combines these two approaches – with the whole class working in the Hall (or drama room) on a regular basis and small groups working for shorter periods in the classroom.

Intervening in the children's own dramatic play and structuring play-corner activities

The simplest way of starting is by intervening (sometimes very briefly) in play-corner activities, taking on a role yourself in the children's own play. This intervention can be as simple as:

- buying items from a shopping list and needing change;
- having a cup of tea and asking questions about the neighbours – 'Is the old man next door still poorly? He really appreciated it when you got his shopping for him last week.'

Even at its simplest, your intervention

- supports the children in their role play;
- introduces the idea that you, the teacher, can play a role yourself;
- creates possibilities for language development;
- creates possibilities for introducing some work in other curriculum areas (e.g. counting);
- encourages them to think beyond the immediate, maybe introducing simple notions of cause and effect narrative;
- gives you the opportunity to introduce simple signals indicating when you are in and out of role, thereby accustoming them to this strategy for when you use it later in a whole group drama.

To those children who find any sort of role play difficult (perhaps because it has been discouraged at home, or because they are shy) it communicates to them that you approve of such play. As they get used to your interventions, you can make them more challenging. Perhaps, instead of asking questions about the neighbours, you can yourself be the old person who lives next door:

> 'I know you're very busy (acknowledging and supporting what they're already doing) but I wonder if you could help me? I've been very poorly and I can't get out to the shops. Can you help me make a shopping list?'

When intervening in this way with a small group working on their own in the play-corner you'll need to think through how much time you can afford to give them. How long can you leave the rest of the class to get on with their own work? You'll need to be clear about the purpose of your intervention. Is it:

- to challenge?
- to support?
- to focus?
- to stimulate?

In practice, it is often a combination of these. If the children are already working well, perhaps all you need to do is to present them with a stimulus: 'I'm trying to arrange a birthday party for my nieces and nephews; could you help me organise it.'

A stimulus to imaginative play

With very young children, an effective way of getting imaginative play started is to put 'something magic' into the play area: 'Here's a magic box. I wonder if you can find out how it works, what it does?' The magic box could equally well be a key, a trinket, a crystal – or even a saucepan. This approach is particularly useful when their play has become 'stuck', when they continue to enact the same situation in the same way.

I once said to a small group of Reception children working in the play area: 'I've heard that this bracelet has some strange magic powers. Could you find out what they are? It doesn't seem to work for me.' I let them get on with it, and returned ten minutes later to find them 'space-walking'. The bracelet not only made them fly, but had taken them to the moon.

You might also try: 'This magic chair seems to make people who sit in it very grumpy. It's not supposed to do that at all. Can you help me put it right?'

Note that the basic approach with very young children is in many ways similar to that we use with other age groups: I, the teacher, do *not* know. Can you help me. You will need to spend longer with children who find role play itself difficult, or who will work alone but not with others. Simply entering and offering a stimulus can provoke argument, disagreement and even tears. Taking on a role yourself and making that role the focus of the dramatic play enables you to support contributions as they're made. When you have some children who find it difficult to work with others, one solution is to work with smaller groups – maybe even just two children at a time for five minutes or so.

Using an item of costume can be a powerful stimulus to initiate dramatic play. *A well-stocked dressing-up box* is a valuable resource. Hats, caps and headgear of various kinds are useful because they are so easy to use quickly and without fuss; but make sure it also contains plenty of different fabrics and textiles as well as props and items of clothing. In this way they are not only using the clothes in the box but also using textiles and fabrics creatively. I tend to use the dressing-up box as a resource which the children can go to during their own dramatic play, although it can become distracting if the children want to use it when you're working as a whole group; and you will need to establish clear rules about when it can and cannot be accessed.

Whole group work

So far I've described what might be called a 'gently, gently' approach. It not only gives the inexperienced teacher an opportunity to build up confidence, it also gets children used to role play being taken seriously. The problem with using small group work with young children is that it can be rather disparate: they will happily play for long periods, but find it difficult to share each other's work unless there is a powerful dramatic context, as provided by whole group work, which gives us the chance to focus the drama. In whole group drama we can work with the class to create a story in which they all have a stake, slowing it down at particular moments, thereby creating strong dramatic tension, deepening understanding and also enabling us to value publicly the contribution of particular children.

The two ways of working (in small groups and in a whole class group) are not mutually exclusive. As discussed in Chapter 2, whole group work only occasionally means the whole class doing the same thing at the same time. It's more useful to think of it as a way of giving coherence and focus to the work of small groups.

Example

The Magician Who Lost His Magic

David McKee is probably best known for the ever popular *Not Now Bernard* and the series about *Elmer* the patchwork elephant. *The Magician Who Lost His Magic*, the first of a series about Melric the Magician, is now out of print, but is a wonderful book, and very stimulating for drama. It tells the story of how Melric woke up one day to find he no longer had any magic. Everyone in the castle where he lives had become totally reliant on him to do everything for them, so the loss of the magic is disastrous. In the story Melric goes off on a quest to various fellow magicians to seek help. In a drama sparking off from the book you can change the dramatic frame and look at the story from the point of view of the people in the castle.

- What's happening in the castle kitchens?

- How does everyone manage?

You can break into small groups and look at what's happening throughout the castle. The pictures in the book are a useful stimulus because they hint at the disasters and yet allow the children to flesh out the world of the carpenters, the gardeners, the cooks, the soldiers, the furniture makers (perhaps using small pieces of fabric to indicate who they are). Children love acting out 'disasters'. From here you could go on to explore how the people in the castle manage without Melric. Frequently young children use 'magic' as a way of solving problems, and thereby avoiding the drama. This story itself offers a useful control device in that you're asking them how they manage without magic.

Here are some brief alternative suggestions:

- Class as nearby townspeople who have never had the dubious benefit of Melric's magic. Teacher (in role) goes to them to seek advice: 'Melric, our magician, has lost all his magic; and we don't know how to do anything. We don't even know how to boil a kettle. Could I stay with you for a few days and learn how you manage without magic?'

- My name is Mertel; I'm Melric's sister. I've heard that my brother has been wasting his magic. If we're to help him get his magic back I'm going to need to know just what he's been up to.

The dramatic frame

This example illustrates how we can use different dramatic frames to develop drama from story with this age group. As with older children we use the story as the possible starting point, but shift the point of view, so that they are not simply acting out what they have heard – but, rather, making decisions which affect the drama.

Shifting the dramatic frame enables us to use the dramatic fictions with which the children are familiar as starting points for drama, while still developing original, imaginative work. 'We're going to make up a play together. It's going to have Melric in it, but it'll be our play . . . .' There is something very appealing about this to children: it offers them the pleasure of exploring a fictional world with which they are already familiar, whilst at the same time making their own contribution to it.

Example

The Circus

When I first started teaching drama the stock Infant lesson was 'making a circus'! Times have changed, as have circuses and public attitudes towards them. Not many children are likely to have been to a circus; but although they're not as glamorous or as attractive as they once were, they still hold a fascination for children.

If we're going to use The Circus as the theme for our drama we need to consider another dramatic frame than simply putting together all the different acts, for example, the teacher in role produces a large document with the title *Last Will and Testament*. 'My dear old Uncle Billy died recently and I've inherited his circus. I've got to run it and I don't know anything about circuses. What's worse is that before he died all the people who looked after the animals had left and got jobs with other circuses. All the animals are in their cages, but they don't seem to have much space, and some of them haven't been fed properly for a long time. I need your help and advice.' The drama is about how to look after the animals, finding out what they eat, where they come from, maybe whether we can release them back into the wild.

Organisation

One of the problems often associated with working with young children is their apparently short concentration span. That does not mean that we should not attempt serious drama work with them, but that we need to give careful thought in our planning to the appropriateness of the material. Exactly the same principles apply as with any age group. We need to catch and hold their attention. The best way of doing that is with strong images; by intriguing them, by creating tense dramatic moments. To this end teacher-in-role work with young children is especially effective.

Pretend and reality

There is a danger in letting the drama become too real for young children. We don't want the dragons and giants of the drama to follow them home and give them nightmares. We need to remind children that what we're doing in drama is pretending. This is another reason that I deliberately choose to move frequently in and out of role in drama with young children, and why I often use the strategy of asking them to help me create (or construct) the character that I play. It is also important to create clear endings for each drama session, so that when they leave the hall or the drama room those elements of the drama that have been potentially frightening can be left safely behind.

Discussions

However dramatic and intriguing you make the work, however visual, there will be times when you need to sit down with them and talk things through. These periods of reflection and decision making are important, but we must not let them get out of hand. Discussion is only of interest to those participating in it, and many young children find it extremely difficult to articulate their ideas verbally – especially before they've actually done what you're talking about.

I tackle the problem by trying to act on suggestions as soon as they're made – any discussion occurs after the action.

We have a problem. We need to discuss it. Draw the children to you; take them into your confidence. You'll have to use more than words to convince them just how special they are in this process. You clarify the problem as visually as possible; and then you get ten different solutions shouted out. What do you do? You act on one of them at a time, and then decide which, if any, is going to be most productive.

The giant's toothache

In advance of the drama session I've made several large sweet papers. When they come into the Hall they see these giant wrappers leading to the corner of the room. We talk about why they might be there; who they might belong to. They're all pretty certain that they belong to a giant.

I ask them: 'Do they want to meet the giant.' They do. 'What will he be like?' We construct the character of the giant; a child makes a suggestion, and we all have a go at enacting it, seeing what it would look like. How does he walk? They show me. I pick up on one idea at a time, and we try each of these as a group. I try it myself, to see if I've got the right idea. How does he talk? How does he eat? They want a frightening giant, big and loud and angry.

I then ask if they're ready to meet the giant. They are; and he's pretty much the way they'd constructed him, except that he's in the corner, bent over and moaning. They gather round, tentatively asking what's wrong. I point to my mouth and my tummy.

I come out of role and ask them about what they've seen. What do they know about the giant? They tell me he's got toothache and tummy ache from eating too many sweets. They want to help him, and I have to remind them that he might be frightening (that was the way they had wanted him to be) so we'll need to approach him very carefully. (This adds to the dramatic tension.) So the issue becomes: How do we help a giant who is poorly, but who might get very angry with us if we annoy him?

As you'd expect with this age group, there is an immediate barrage of responses. 'Clean his teeth for him', says one child. With older children we might spend some time discussing this (perhaps wondering if the giant would ever let us get near enough to open his mouth and clean his teeth for him); with this age group, however, I immediately enthuse about the idea: 'Right, that's really good. But aren't we going to need a very large toothbrush. We'll have to make that ourselves. Go to the shops and buy anything you think would be useful to make a giant's toothbrush . . . .' And then, when we've bought all the materials and made the giant's toothbrush (which could itself be a Technology task), that's when I go back into role as the giant and refuse to let them come anywhere near me with their (mimed) toothbrush.

I come out of role again and ask them what we should do. One child suggests we give him a bath. You can see how firmly grounded the drama is in their own reality. So we have to make the bath tub and then fill it with water. It needs to be hot water, so we have to be careful . . . . And the drama continues in this way: a stimulus to excite and intrigue; a problem; action and then thought about the action. Action and then reflection. People frequently get into difficulties with this age group by trying to think through the consequences of suggestions before trying them out, which requires an inappropriately sophisticated level of thought on the part of the children.

Magic

Several of these examples refer to 'magic' in some way. In drama magic is both a blessing and a curse; a blessing because it creates a wonderful control device, and because it can be stimulating to the imagination; a curse because children can – and often do – use it as a way of saying 'This is not a problem', using magic to get them out of seeking a solution.

Magic as a control device

When working with young children it is sometimes a good idea to invoke magic: 'When we go into the Hall we are going through a magic door', as if it were a door to a magic wardrobe. You can say that if they don't keep to the agreed rules of the drama, then the magic will start to fail; if they climb up the wall bars when you have asked them not to, you can say that the magic only works when their feet are touching the ground, thus using the fiction of the drama to limit the space they work in and remind them through a dramatic device of those rules which you will have agreed before the lesson begins.

The Hall, the drama itself, becomes magic. Anything can happen, as long as the rules of the magic are adhered to. Using the device of the 'magic door' also allows you to contain the world of pretend within the hall if, for example, there are children in the class for whom the drama frequently becomes too real.

The curse of magic

Anybody who has taught Drama with Primary school children will have come across many examples of magic being used as a 'Get out'. For example:

■ We're stuck in a cave. There's been a rock fall. There seems to be no way out. At which point a child says, 'It's alright, I've brought a magic spade with me. It can dig us out in ten seconds.' You could, of course, reply, 'Nonsense, there are no such things as magic spades' (and I've been tempted often enough); but that could be dismissive, and there's a good chance that the child who offers the spade is doing so in good faith.

Instead, try: 'Thank goodness you've brought that. How marvellous', and then start asking questions about the magic:

■ 'How long does the magic last?'

■ 'What are the dangers of using it?'

■ 'Where did you get it? It's not stolen, is it?'

Enter into the world of the magic, accept the idea, but challenge it: use the magic, but create limitations for it. Establish the parameters. What does the magic spade do exactly? When does it, and when does it not work? By giving the magic limitations, asking in which particular circumstances it works, the drama is actually enhanced. The children have to make a decision about using the magic, they have to think when would be a good time to use it and when would be harmful.

In this respect the following is a technique which I have found particularly useful:

■ We're stuck (again)! It doesn't matter where. The problem is how to get away from the encroaching flood water. A child says she has brought a Magic Carpet. 'How wonderful. Can I look at it? Oh it's magnificent isn't it . . . . A bit small, but beautifully coloured. Oh, what's this? A label?' And then I 'read' aloud: 'MAGIC CARPET. DANGER. DO NOT USE EXCEPT . . . .' 'Oh dear. The rest of the label's been torn.'

We're exploring the world of exciting new technology. It's magic, of course, and it brings great benefit to us but it could also have terrible dangers in store for us – just like magic carpets! The focus of the drama shifts to discovering the dangers, and weighing up pros and cons of using the magic carpet.

Avoiding the problem

There are times, of course, when one simply feels it is inappropriate to be dealing with magic; and 'magic' can take many forms, including laser guns which appear from nowhere.

It is important to establish at the beginning of a drama lesson/project whether magic is to be allowed or not. If it is agreed that there is to be *no* magic, the teacher and the children must stick by their decision.

Before any sort of an expedition – be it to South America, or a distant star – I often ask the children to make a list of all the things they will be taking with them. This becomes an important task in itself, and can be done either in the hall or in the classroom (perhaps in role). With older children it could be that each child makes his/her own list on a piece of paper; with younger children maybe we do it as a class, and the teacher writes everything on the blackboard; or perhaps nothing is written down by individuals, with each giving what they will need to the teacher who's a 'Quartermaster'. The lists could be written or sketched. Maybe some of the items have to be purchased.

What matters is that a limitation has been set; and *now* if a child brings out a gun, a knife, a rope ladder or even a box of matches you can check with the list and then either stay in role and say 'You may have meant to bring that rope ladder, but it's not here', *or* come out of role and discuss the agreed rules of the drama, one of which is perhaps that in *this* drama there is no recourse to magic. The lists have been agreed, and anything not on the list cannot simply 'appear' from nowhere.

Still image and Forum Theatre with young children

Most of the ideas, techniques and strategies described in Part 1 hold good for working with young children, but it is worth devoting time to a specific discussion of how one might adapt the work on still image and Forum Theatre for use with this age group, as they are sometimes thought to be strategies that can only be successfully used with older children.

Still images

Reception children are used to stories told in the form of consecutive images through comic strips; they're also familiar with 'freeze frame' on video. A simple way of introducing still image work with this age group is to have them walk or run round the hall and then stop and freeze at a given signal. You say you'll try to lift up the child who is stillest. We can then look at one or two of the still images as if they were statues or models in a theme park. Perhaps we then go on and create a drama about a theme park. Maybe the class are model makers; they could make still images of their favourite cartoon characters.

Consider two images:

1. children taking apples from a tree;
2. a farmer shouting at the children.

In this order it's a story of crime and punishment. If we reverse the order we get a story of revenge, the children getting their own back. Working with the images develops the concept of cause and effect in narrative – an important early stage in teaching about narrative. We can do the work by using photographs or drawings initially, but it's often more exciting for the children to make the images themselves, perhaps later drawing what they have done in comic strip form and making their own comic based on the story that's been created in the drama.

Forum Theatre

Obviously, you cannot leave children to work independently or in small groups, but much of the best drama work is collaborative, and that is one of the keys to successful work with young children; one of the reasons that Forum Theatre can easily be applied to working with young children.

'The giant's toothache' shows how we might use forum theatre to construct a character, a technique which is useful with all ages. By giving young children the opportunity to create the more 'dangerous' characters themselves, they are made safe; the elements of pretend are made clearer. They like their drama to be exciting, but if it is to be frightening, they need to feel in control of their fear. The technique of constructing a character in this way is one which is wonderfully adaptable. Suppose we need a dragon in a drama. If we're going to stick by the principle outlined above of keeping close to the centre of the action, we'll need to meet the dragon, to find out what it's really like, maybe to persuade it to come and melt an iceberg for drinking water.

How do we create a dragon? Ask the children. 'If you like, I'll pretend to be the dragon, but you'll have to help me. How can I do it? Have you seen the dragon? Can you show me what it looks like? My arms aren't big enough to be wings; what can I use for wings? Is there anything in the dressing-up box that looks like dragon skin? And what about its face?'

Having gone through this process, and perhaps used various bits of PE apparatus to create the dragon's lair, maybe ask the children to shut their eyes and imagine the dragon in its lair, talking them through the suggestions they've made, helping them to visualise their creation, before taking on the role. When you take on the role, though, always hold something in reserve, so it's what they've created, but here's something unexpected about it. Maybe the dragon's lost its old fire, maybe it's an endangered species, maybe it's rather timid . . . . Be careful with your questioning. Don't ask questions to which you don't want answers. If you want a fireless dragon, don't ask them if the dragon breathes fire.

Fantasy and the power of story

There are several schools of thought about whether young children get more from working on what they know – dramas about shopping, going to school, their daily routines – or fantasy. My own feeling is that we need to start where children feel most comfortable, and then to introduce elements which are better described as mythic rather than fantastic; that is, to dramatise or create stories which contain imagery and symbolism which is likely to excite the children, and yet which they can relate to their own lives. I'm sure that young children like stories about giants so much because that's what adults seem like to them. Dealing with dragons (or aliens) in drama is an enjoyable and safe way of dealing with our fears. In all these dramas the children's responses are a way of exploring their relationship with the world they know – as we've seen in 'The giant's toothache'.

Chapter 5 contains embedded examples of two drama projects undertaken with Reception children, 'The Giant Awakes' and 'The Crashed Space Ship'. The discussion of 'Drama and story' in Chapter 1 also contains a number of practical examples which are well suited for use with children in Early Years.

2 Drama in an integrated curriculum

It's not difficult to see how role play and drama can be used to achieve many of the learning objectives for Speaking, Listening and Responding in the Primary Framework for literacy. What is less obvious is that drama can have a central role in developing children's reading and writing skills, and that it can be a powerful force for motivating and enhancing work in every curriculum area. While it takes ingenuity and careful thought, it is possible and productive to use drama at the *centre* of the curriculum, rather than as an occasional extra. This part of the book explores how drama can be used alongside other subjects; how it can be used to create and enhance learning opportunities, to stimulate research, and to give cross-curricular coherence. It examines in detail the specific possibilities created by writing in role; and then moves on to examine specific examples of cross-curricular work.

Content

5
Drama in an integrated curriculum

This chapter is concerned with using drama to encourage and motivate learning and to create coherence between different curriculum areas. It contains four embedded examples of such work throughout the primary age range.

- Writing in role
- Reading in role
- Meaning beyond the literal
- Drama and other subject areas
- Maps
- Drama in topic work

Embedded examples:

- *The Crashed Spaceship*
- *The Giant Awakes*
- *The Iron Age Encampment*
- *The Arrival*

It has been argued that using drama as a learning medium in some way detracts from the power of drama itself. This is a flawed and misguided argument which indicates a failure to understand the nature of drama, which is *essentially* cross-disciplinary. You cannot have drama which does not refer to other curriculum areas. All drama has to have content; it has to be *about* something. Furthermore, drama in schools is greatly enhanced by the work that can accompany it in other curriculum areas. You can use drama without specifically teaching about dramatic forms (although in using drama as a learning medium, you cannot help but make use of dramatic forms), but you cannot effectively teach anything about the nature of dramatic forms without some sort of content.

In Early Years, for example, children's activities in the role-play area frequently include shopping. It would be wasteful not to make use of the children's interest in their dramatic play to set tasks within their play which challenge them to do some work on counting and simple Maths.

Cross-curricular links between drama and other subject areas can be passive, as when, for example, children act out stories that have been read to them without taking any decisions of their own; or they can be active: when you structure the drama in such a way that it enables the children to make decisions, then the drama leaps off from the springboard of the story rather than being tied passively to predetermined decisions. The problem of passive links is that at best they waste, and at worst deny, all kinds of learning opportunities. In a similar way, simply asking children to draw a picture of what happened in their drama wastes opportunities to move the drama forward and make the art work purposeful: when the pictures that they make are given significance within the drama, the quality of both the drama and the art work improves. Active cross-fertilisation is in itself exciting and highly productive. The commitment to the drama becomes greater, and the work in other curriculum areas is tackled with real purpose.

Drama lends itself to becoming part of topic work because

- it gives you *content* for your drama work;
- it animates topic work;
- it facilitates continuity within a drama project;
- it makes it easier to do drama in other spaces than the school hall.

By linking your drama and your topic work, you can take ten or fifteen minutes at various times during the day to work with small groups. If the whole class is involved in researching a topic – which might include using the computer, browsing through the library, watching a video programme, or even (as older children become more confident) working with original historical documents –

it becomes easier to supervise the work of one small group (that might, for example, be preparing an interview) while the rest of the class work independently on related activities.

If the narrative of the drama continues from one day to the next, it makes sense to do at least some drama in the classroom most days. If you use Forum Theatre, or interrogate some still image presentations, you don't even need to push the desks back. It's possible to use classroom time for discussions and all the out of role preparatory work that greatly strengthens the children's commitment to drama.

The guiding principles in using drama alongside other curriculum areas are that it should:

- give greater purpose and meaning to work both in drama and in associated curriculum areas;
- create an appetite for research of all kinds;
- create opportunities for the children to give their work authenticity;
- create contexts in which the relationship between the different curriculum areas is strengthened.

The clear implication of these principles is that cross-curricular work should be interactive, rather than tangential; if the work in other curriculum areas is to be purposeful, it must have a clear purpose within the context of the drama. Some of this work will take place in the classroom, some of it during drama time. It can be done in or out of role – with the information gathered through research, for example, then used to inform the subsequent drama.

Writing in role

The developing fiction of whole group drama demands a range of different kinds of work from the children. Much of this work will be writing in role of one kind or another. This can range from emergent writing (as exemplified in 'The Crashed Spaceship' below and 'The Giant Awakes' below) to sophisticated petitions whose wording needs to be carefully worked on and formalised. Writing in role slows the drama down in productive fashion, encouraging children to look at a particular situation in greater depth than they would otherwise; but it also gives context and purpose to writing.

Whenever we look at children's writing, we should try to respond to the content, but this can sometimes be difficult; children themselves often become over-anxious about the surface features of their writing and frightened of making mistakes. By making written work of all kinds (including Maths, Science, IT and Artwork) a part of their drama we provide a sort of safety net, a 'No Penalty Zone' in which they can pretend to be someone other than themselves writing their letter, wording their advertisement or drawing up their menu. The motivation to write is heightened, and writing of great diversity can be encouraged – including, where appropriate, writing in the child's own language or dialect.

To summarise, writing in role can provide opportunities for children to:

- write under the protective shield of a role;
- write for a specific (albeit imagined) reader;
- write in different voices;
- experiment with vocabulary, speech patterns, rhythm and vocabulary language tones and registers;
- write for purpose;
- write to effect change.

Writing in role is likely to be most effective and most empowering for children when it arises within the fiction of the drama, and in response to the needs of specific situations. A given situation might demand a letter or a text or a document to be created; but writing in role is also likely to include:

- advertisements
- census returns
- CVs
- diagrams
- diaries
- directions
- documents
- drawings
- instructions
- interviews
- inventories
- journals
- labels and signs
- letters

- lists
- maps
- memoranda
- messages in code
- newspaper reports, headlines
- posters
- tickets.

Reading in role

Teachers are well aware of the need to value children's work. Valuing art work usually means displaying it. In the case of posters, labels or signs written in role, display is appropriate; but having asked children to write in role, we should consider how might we *respond in role*; how the writing they have produced can be valued within the dramatic fiction. This enables children to see their writing having an effect; and also moves the drama forward, and enhances it. It's important to honour and respect the work that children produce, giving it significance on its own terms.

Examples

The two examples below are accounts of work undertaken with reception classes (both of which had some experience of drama and were used to the teacher in role strategy); one in a rural school, one in an inner-city multi-racial school.

The Crashed Spaceship

We begin by talking about the children's daily routine of coming to school and returning home, which they enact individually and in pairs. I then tell them a story which they act out: one day the children all set off home only to find that a great big hole has opened up in the playground. I ask them to form a circle, as if standing around the hole, and then to close their eyes, warning them that when they open their eyes again, I shall be playing a part in the drama.

▶

When I ask them to open their eyes, I am in the middle of the circle, as if at the bottom of the hole, wearing a pair of very dark goggles, clearly in role, but as what? A tense moment! We wait a little and then I step out of role, remove the goggles, and ask them what they think they have seen. The children decide that it is an alien creature. Two children climb down into the hole (having first borrowed a rope ladder!) and try to talk to 'the creature'. I make this a little difficult, creating an opportunity to encourage a shy child to communicate with the alien. She discovers that the alien's space ship has crashed. 'Can you help me find all the pieces?' I ask.

They draw the pieces and label their drawings. Many of the children are not yet able to write in conventional form, but all tackle the task of labelling the various (imaginary) bits and pieces of the space ship. The labelling matters; without it they cannot rebuild the alien's space ship. I am able to respond to their *emergent writing* honestly and give it significance in the drama. 'I can't make this out', I say (as myself, not the alien), to which several children respond: 'No, that's because it's written in the alien's language.' So the labels now need to be 'translated', and this becomes a collaborative process with children of different abilities working together. One child says his labels are in English, and they can't be read easily because they're in grown-up, joined-up writing!

Writing and labelling is at the heart of this drama; and the resulting work is of a very high standard, with several children who have recently joined the school writing something for the first time.

The Giant Awakes

I begin by telling the children a story about a giant who was very unpopular with all the other giants because he wouldn't eat people or animals. I ask the children what his name might be; they decide on 'Herbert Thunder'. With each of them individually playing Herbert Thunder, they act out the first part of the story: Herbert finds a lonely spot for himself, and there he cries himself to sleep. His tears form rivers. Once he is asleep, he sleeps for a very long time – for thousands of years. While he is asleep, leaves fall on him and turn into soil.

It's not until the present day that the giant wakes up and tries to dig his way to the surface. He looks for food. The children act out each of these actions individually, with me asking them *how* he might do each of the actions; and thus they begin to start making decisions which affect the outcome of the drama, and create a sense of their ownership of it.

While looking for food they are careful not to eat animals or human beings. I ask them what he might like eating; some suggest eating car tyres and drinking oil (echoes of Ted Hughes' *The Iron Man* here). Herbert heads for a nearby town where, having gorged himself in a garage, he finds his way to an open space and falls asleep.

Up to this point the children have all been acting as the giant. I gather the class and ask if they are now willing to play grown-ups. They are keen to do so, and become the townspeople. I take on the role of the Mayor to ask – 'What on earth has been causing all this damage?' The townspeople say it is a giant; but the Mayor doesn't believe them. He wants proof: 'A giant indeed. There are no such things. I'll have to see some pictures or photographs that show me just how big he really is.'

Figure 5.1 Herbert Thunder

The children draw and paint their representations of the giant. Several show the giant beside trees, some next to buildings; one remarkable painting (Figure 5.1) has Herbert with his head in the clouds!

The Mayor is convinced, and wonders what they should do next. The townspeople decide to write letters to the giant asking him to leave, reasoning that talking to him directly would be too dangerous. They set about this task with great enthusiasm. The Mayor asks them to tell him what has been written because there are several which he cannot read. The children explain that these have been written in the giant's own language (again, emergent writing). As in 'The Crashed Spaceship', this is the first time that several of the children have produced written work since arriving in the school.

The examples above are relatively simple, but they exemplify the way that drama stimulates and motivates work in other curriculum areas (in this case writing and art work); and how that work then becomes vital to the development of the drama.

The brief list of writing-in-role activities below indicates some further avenues you might want to explore:

Diaries

- journals
- ship's log
- starship's log.

Letters

informal:

- to Mum, Dad, grandparents, brothers, sisters
- to friends, pen friend
- from Jack at the top of the beanstalk.

formal:

- pleas for forgiveness/mercy
- requests for planning permission
- requests that the selfish giant let people play in his garden
- from the Mayor of Hamelin to the Pied Piper
- petitions (for the release of the children of Hamelin).

Messages

- telegrams
- memoranda
- messages in code
- reports from spaceship to Earth via computer
- messages in a bottle after a shipwreck.

Lists

- inventory of furniture in a Haunted House;
- inventory of equipment to take on a journey or expedition;
- menus for the celebratory banquet or a friend's birthday party;
- shopping list for ingredients for a cake;
- shopping list for Christmas presents;
- census returns – who lives here, what do they do?

Advertisements

- classified to put in newspaper/magazine;
- For sale/wanted;
- 'REWARD offered to anyone who dares to stay overnight in the Haunted House?'
- 'Lost – one dragon!' personal card in shop window;
- display advertisements/posters.

Scripts

- transcripts of interviews for radio, TV, newspapers.

Newspaper reports

- by reporters who saw the children of Hamelin piped away;
- by eye-witnesses who have seen the giant eating car tyres.

Headlines

- newspapers;
- magazines;
- TV/radio programmes.

Database

- details of the crew on the space ship;
- details of wild life survey by conservation workers.

Plans

- designs for a conservation area;
- diagrams of how to put the alien's space ship back together;

- to prevent anyone else climbing up the beanstalk and stealing things from us;
- map of the giant's castle, showing how we might set Jack free;
- town plan of Hamelin.

Much of this written work can be done alone, but some of it is best achieved by working in small teams or collaboratively as a whole class: it might be, for example, that the purpose of the drama is to work together to produce documents, which will later be used as part of the drama, for example:

- letters written by the sailors on the *Mary Rose* as they left port;
- wording of a peace treaty;
- an agreement between the people of Hamelin and the Pied Piper;
- Rules of Space: how do we behave on our (or the alien's) space ship?

As elsewhere in the book these suggestions are not intended to be prescriptive but, rather, a stimulus for ideas. Here are some brief ideas as to how some of the Pied Piper suggestions might work in practice:

- After the story has been read to the class, children might take on roles as the townspeople of Hamelin. The teacher as the Mayor asks for their help. Who saw the children being lured away? What did the newspapers/radio/TV say about it? What should the Mayor write to the Pied Piper? Can the towns-people help with the letter(s)? How do we deliver the resulting letter(s) to the Pied Piper?
- Teacher takes on role of the Pied Piper and tells the class (as townspeople) that if they write letters to their children s/he will deliver them to the children. Out of role, the teacher could suggest these might contain coded escape plans.
- The Pied Piper is never actually seen; all communication is by letter or petition – with the teacher writing replies but not actually appearing in the role.
- In any of these, the life of the town could be built up through various activities including role-play, mime, map making, art work. Making a town plan can be done with young children by suggesting the children draw pictures of different parts of the town and sticking these onto a large piece of paper which will go on the hall or classroom wall.

Meanings beyond the literal

'It is one of those curious facts that when two things are compared in a metaphor we see both of them . . . more distinctly . . . .'

Ted Hughes (1967: 45)

In some ways all drama and theatre creates meanings beyond the literal. We never read any theatrical event at only one level – whether it is a performance in the National Theatre or an improvised exchange in the role-play area of an infant classroom. When most pre-school children engage in dramatic play, they use toys to stand in for people, they configure an imaginative representation of their world using whatever they can find. Not only do most children get great pleasure from their metaphorical representations of their world, it is an important way for them to explore their interaction with it. Young children understand and love the monster in David McKee's *Not Now Bernard* because the book offers a witty and a safe way of exploring 'monstrous' behaviour. The metaphorical framework provides a protective shield from the difficulties of confronting such issues in the real world, whilst simultaneously allowing us to explore them in depth.

Metaphorical meanings are not fixed, they change and they exist in the spaces between us; they are never simply created by 'makers' and understood by 'responders'; they are a product of our interactions with each other and with our culture and our environment. Understanding and learning to play with this fluidity must be central to drama and, indeed, to any education which values creativity, which styles itself as humanising.

In my experience, children in the Early Years are more than capable of exploring and manipulating metaphor and symbol. Returning to the example of *Jack and the Beanstalk*, one has only to ask questions which explore the different values that different people place on things to open up issues of meaning beyond the literal: 'What does the cow mean to Jack and his Mum?' 'What do the beans mean to them?' With Year 1 children you may not use the terminology of metaphors and symbols, but that is what your questioning is getting at. The beans might thus be a symbol of Jack's idleness or gullibility – or of hope, of new life, of independence.

Many of the examples in this book are rich in metaphor and symbol. In every case, however, the teacher needs to be ready to tease out the non-literal meanings. Below are some simple practical ways of thinking about developing meaning beyond the literal.

Objects

Consider some of the different meanings contained in the way we use a *key*:

- opening doors, containers or gates that have long been locked:
  'Are you sure you want to do this? We may find things that are best kept locked away.'

- locking doors or containers:
  'Are you sure we've got everything?'
- throwing the key away:
  'This really will mean no going back. I turn this key and . . .'
- transferring ownership:
  'It's yours now. That's a great deal of responsibility.'

A cloak can be used:

- to conceal identity or disguise;
- to give warmth and protection;
- to signify power; and assume or transfer it.

A loaf of bread can be:

- divided between everybody or refused to someone as punishment;
- snatched or stolen;
- part of a ceremony or ritual.

An empty bowl can:

- signify hunger and poverty;
- be a gift from a skilled craftsperson.

A rope can:

- bind us together as we make our journey through the secret caves;
- create a *Time Line*, whereby we create a visual representation of someone's life history on the floor of the Hall.

Actions

Delivering a letter can be both a very ordinary action and one which is rich in symbolic significance, providing the teacher draws out the meaning. In 'The Coming of the Railway' (pp. 204–13), for example, an old man (teacher in role) refuses to sell his house to the railway company. Everybody else in the town wants the railway, and if he doesn't sell, the company will choose an alternative route. The Council (of children) has agreed to effect a compulsory purchase. The class can simply tell him he has to go, but the moment of eviction is potentially highly charged and to let it slip by is to waste opportunities. If the Council choose someone to act as Bailiff, the act of serving the eviction order on the old man (*delivering a letter*) becomes a highly charged dramatic moment. Because it carries deep symbolic resonance it will be memorable, dramatic and open up rich opportunities for discussion.

Consider how the following actions are both 'ordinary', and symbolic:

- Giving someone a mug of water
  Suppose that person is a stranger who has been perceived as a threat, but is now evidently very weak . . . .
  Suppose s/he is suspected of carrying a highly infectious illness . . . .

- Tearing up a letter
  Suppose we are US Cavalry and the letters contain orders to attack a Native American village . . . .
  'It's easy to tear up the letter. It's what happens now that worries me.'

- Putting up or taking down a poster
  Suppose it offers a large reward for the arrest of a smuggler, who is our neighbour . . . .

In each case, the teacher's job is to tease out meanings, partly through her own reflection on decisions and action, partly through asking questions that enable the children to see the range of meanings contained in their own work. It is in those meanings that transcend the literal that the most powerful links between different areas of the curriculum can be made – because the Maths, the History, the Science and Technology become essential parts of human stories that have been created by the children with whom we're collaborating.

Drama and other subject areas

Many of the practical examples given in this book contain reference to work in other curriculum areas. The following brief notes are indications as to how one might use drama both to stimulate and support work in specific curriculum areas.

Maths

- *Map making, co-ordinates, scale, contours*
  The drama begins with the children being shown a treasure map. How do we read it? Can we plan a route?
  The children make their own maps or plans. The situation demands that they find a way of representing scale and height.

- *Calculation*
  How is food to be rationed – on a journey; an expedition; during a siege?

We're stuck in our space ship. How do we calculate the volume of air left? And how long will this last us?

Working out wages and bonuses, or taxes owing.

- *IT Databases*
  Inventories of equipment;
  List of crew members (ship, submarine, space ship) with country of origin, age, interests, training, previous experience, years' service.

- *Graphs*
  Bar graphs to record results of research into community prior to building of new leisure centre / road / railway station.

- *Codes*
  The space ship and crew trapped on a distant planet. We need to send messages in code so they cannot be understood by aliens; or break the coded messages (created by the teacher) they are receiving from the alien inhabitants.

Science, Design and Technology

- *Flight*
  We are in the mountains, on an expedition / fleeing a tyrant / trying to find somewhere safe to live after an earthquake has destroyed our town; we come to a ravine. We need to get a message to the people on the other side. A flying machine? A paper dart? What design will fly furthest and straightest?

- *Life on Earth*
  Space voyagers who have discovered a 'sister planet' to Earth, or time travellers returning to the present day from the future, or aliens planning a visit to Earth. In each of these cases the task is to find out what life on Earth is really like. This could be a way of introducing study of skeletons, use of a microscope to compare animal and human hair. This idea of making the world with which we are familiar seem strange to us, and thereby increasing our curiosity about it, is one which theatre practitioners will be familiar with through the work of Bertolt Brecht. See also *Media Studies*, below.

- *Food preservation*
  A long voyage by sea in a sailing ship (as pirates, emigrants, smugglers, Navy). How will we keep food from going off without the use of refrigerators? What food will be good to take with us?

- *Design*
  Teacher requests children's help, as experts, in designing a supermarket, pet shop – plans and model making.

Shipwrecked on an island with limited resources. We need to make a boat to get off. What could we make it out of? How do we make it?

Geography

- *Population movements* – in a drama about emigration (see example below, *The Arrival*)
- *Ecology and animal origins*
  The teacher (in role) has inherited a badly run circus or zoo. She requests the children's help and advice. What food and bedding should the animals have? How much space? What sort of environment would they enjoy in the wild? Should they be returned to the wild?

Art

- *Drawing, painting*
  Children's art work takes on status of evidence (as in 'The Giant Awakes'). Existing art work (e.g. *Children's Games*) interrogated. Who painted this? Under what circumstances? Drama arouses curiosity about historical and social context of the painting.
- *Photography*
  Mug shots for identity cards or passports;
  Photographs taken of still image work;
  Photographs used as starting points for drama.
- *3D*
  Making the artefacts and sculptures of a given community.

Music

- Making sound pictures using musical instruments and voices but not words – of (for example) a swamp, building site, storm at sea.
- Time / space travellers make audio tapes of the sounds and rhythms they have heard on the voyages – presented to the whole group as part of a debriefing session.
- Using recorded music to create atmosphere. One class could make an atmospheric audio recording, which could then be played back to another class as a way of initiating the drama: 'When you hear this, where do you think we might be?'

Media Studies

- *Alien visitors*

Class as aliens planning a visit to Earth. They study magazines, advertise-ments, television programmes and films to find out what life on Earth will be like and to prepare themselves for their visit. The Media Studies work thus takes place in the context of a dramatic fiction; and the children are encour-aged to see a familiar culture through the eyes of strangers: 'Why do these young humans call their footwear "trainers"?' 'Who are they talking to when they hold these small boxes to their ears?'

History

One of the issues that faces teachers wanting to use drama in the teaching of his-tory is the thorny problem of *facts and authenticity*. What do we do when we're engaged in a drama and the children come up with solutions to problems that are historically inaccurate? The following example illustrates the problem:

Example

The Iron Age Encampment

A class of Year 5 children are working on a project about Iron Age Britain. They have seen pictures of Iron Age encampments, but had done very little previous work on the topic before starting on the drama.

The drama starts with a brief discussion of how people might live without modern technology, and (using the model of the pictures they have seen), they build themselves a fortified encampment – a wonderful image this, with chairs organised into a large circle and then laid down so that the legs all face out, looking as if they are sharpened stakes to deter intruders.

There is lively discussion about the skills that these people are going to need to thrive. These include: hunting, ironworking, woodcutting, clay working, gathering fruits, tending sheep and . . . making honey. They agree on a system of foraging and divide themselves into small skill-based groups. The rules of the encampment are decided upon. We then move into a short period of dramatic play (or 'busy time' as it is sometimes called) in which each of the groups go about their business, which they greatly enjoy – until frustrations start to creep in.

I stop the drama and talk out of role about the problem. I ask each group what they've been doing. When it comes to the turn of the honey makers I ask how they make honey. After a few moments of thought, a child replies 'We collect it from bees.'

'That must be very difficult', say I, admiring. 'How do you do that?' A rather longer silence this time, and then one of the group says hesitantly 'We milk them.'

The rest of the group don't agree, but none of them are sure. They have reached a point in their drama when they need factual information, they want to get it right. So we stop work on the drama for a while and adjourn to the classroom and library, where there are several textbooks about the Iron Age and some encyclopaedias. For half an hour the children research into their own area of work. When they return, each group enthusiastically reports their research findings back to the class.

I am sure that years later those children still remember what they learnt that morning. The drama created a desire, a need for knowledge, which was useful to them – and when they later returned to their drama they were far more committed to it. At the same time they were successfully beginning to develop research skills.

Children have voracious appetites for authenticity, but in drama we should never intimidate them with factual information. We should instead create opportunities which encourage them to seek that information. A child who actively seeks information is likely to make far better use of it than one who passively receives the same information as a chore and is constantly reminded how little s/he knows.

This is not to deny that accuracy is important. It *does* matter that children don't leave a drama lesson believing that Cromwell's army used bazookas and machine guns, but it's important to find the right moment to correct them or, better, to create opportunities for them to discover accurate information for themselves.

Maps

Maps can play a surprisingly important part in the reflective process in drama, making it easier for children to understand the meanings and implications of their work; and also to remember the journeys they have undertaken in the drama: journeys of understanding, emotional journeys, journeys of changing perspectives.

You might start simply by asking the children to draw something on a sheet of paper that they want represented on the map or plan: a house, a shop, the well, the woods . . . . The children's work is more likely to resemble medieval picture maps than an Ordnance Survey sheet. Initially, the activity is a way of *visualising spatial relationships*; a way of representing graphically some of their achievements in the drama. They can either draw their contribution directly onto the paper, or they can stick their drawings onto a large wall map.

Making a storyboard from an everyday journey is a way of visualising a personal chronology, making links between moments, events, decisions or interactions. The storyboard thus becomes a kind of map of a personal journey which marks not geographical or spatial relationships, but those between emotional high spots. I call this an 'emotional map'. Thus an 'emotional map' of a child's walk to school might have five pictures:

- saying goodbye to the dog;
- calling in at the corner shop;
- joking with the lollipop lady as they wait to cross the road;
- dropping a favourite toy in the middle of the road;
- meeting a friend at the school gates.

The concept of visually representing emotional highs and lows can easily be adapted in more complex dramatic fictions; and is as useful with children at top primary as it is with reception infants. It also provides a way of reflecting on drama which draws attention to point of view and makes important links with narrative sequencing. Time lines, emotional maps and storyboards are all ways of reflecting on the drama, and thereby not only deepening the work and broadening perspectives on it, but also developing emotional literacy. The usefulness of the various kinds of mapmaking extends far beyond the obvious curriculum links with maths and geography.

Example

The Arrival

The Arrival by Shaun Tan is a graphic novel about migrants' experiences of leaving the Old Country, travelling across the sea, then arriving and settling in a New World which they find increasingly strange. In Shaun Tan's own words:

A man leaves his wife and child in an impoverished town, seeking better prospects in an unknown country on the other side of a vast ocean . . . . With nothing more than a suitcase and a handful of currency, the immigrant must find a place to live, food to eat and some kind of gainful employment. He is helped along the way by sympathetic strangers, each carrying their own unspoken history: stories of struggle and survival in a world of incomprehensible violence, upheaval and hope.

(Tan 2006 http://www.shauntan.net/books/the-arrival.html accessed January 2009)

There are numerous ways in which you might use the book as a stimulus for drama with children at the upper end of Primary. My book, *Pupils as Playwrights* (Trentham Books, 2008), includes a lengthy chapter exploring various ways of using the book. Here, I'm referring to it in order to give a brief indication of the enormous range of cross-curricular work that a drama based on the book might stimulate; and how the idea of the emotional map can draw different strands of work together. Most of the following ideas could be incorporated into a drama; they could serve to focus reflection, deepen understanding and commitment and move the narrative forwards.

Figure 5.2 Before emigration

In the Old Country (Figure 5.2), before the emigration

- census return, listing those living in a particular street, including details of employment and families;

- map of the area where the emigrants originate;

- lists of items to pack when leaving, and of items to be left behind;

- letter(s) to relative in the New World who has already made the journey;

- letter to be left behind for a friend who has decided to stay in the Old Country;

- drawings reminding emigrant of home;

- emigration documents;

■ diary entries: fears, dreams and hopes for the new life, memories of incidents that brought about the need to emigrate;

■ emotional map and/or time line of the journey undertaken up to the point when they are about to board ship.

On board ship during the voyage to the New World (Figure 5.3)

Figure 5.3 During the voyage

■ notes written to friends and relatives who are being accommodated in another area of the ship;

■ letters written to families and friends in the Old Country;

■ diary entries – conditions on board ship; memories of the Old Country (positive and negative), first sight of the New World;

■ emotional map of the voyage from Old World to New.

At the Port of Entry into the New World (Figure 5.4)

Figure 5.4 Port of entry

■ visas, passports, travel documentation;

■ petition organised by a group of immigrants, requesting that the authorities change their mind about the forced repatriation of one (or more) of their number.

Figure 5.5 Settling in

After settling in the New World (Figure 5.5)

- newspapers headlines and articles about arrival of ship in port;
- Classified Advertisements to put in newspapers or shop windows seeking accommodation and employment (teacher as immigrant seeking help with wording?);
- directions given to new immigrant by a fellow countryman already settled in New World – how to find a place to live, work, food handouts;
- stories told and stories shared with other immigrants;
- census returns – who lives in this block? What employment do they have?
- letters home, trying to assure those left behind that everything is going well; persuading a friend/relative to join them; or warning them not to;
- time line and emotional map of the whole journey.

Drama in topic work

In considering drama's place in topic work, we have to start by thinking how we might dramatise the topic; and that means seeking out human dilemmas, looking for the moments of change in a situation, or the moments when change might be possible; we're looking for those moments when people make choices. In a topic on industrialisation you might, for example, look at the effect of industrialisation on a rural community without work – as in 'The Coming of the Railway' example. There is a difference between easy moralising (which we should avoid) and opening up moral issues. We know (and most children know) that pollution is damaging; that children in Victorian schools were subject to rather repressive regimes; that the slave trade was a bad thing; that being an Ancient Briton after the Romans invaded wasn't nice . . . . But we need to go beyond simplistic simulations. We can do so much more than simply acting as if we were all Victorians. Drama should explore the How and Why of situations.

In a topic about pollution, for example, we might formulate our Key Organising Question as, 'What sort of personal sacrifices might people have to make in order to reduce pollution?' That might lead you to a drama in which the children take on the roles of factory workers who stand to lose their jobs if the factory cleans up its act.

Continuity

Once you start linking drama and topic work you'll find that your drama projects can go on for weeks. You'll need to start thinking about structure and ideas in a slightly different way. While there is no need for each hall lesson to be self-contained, you still need to find strong, engaging starting points. The key to this lies in dramatic tension. Raise the tension, end sessions on a high point so that (rather like a TV serial or a soap opera) everybody wants to know 'What next?'

Topic ideas

The introduction and the section on 'Small group work' in Chapter 2 shows how to set about planning the early stages of a drama lesson. The same approach holds good when planning to use drama as part of a topic. Think about Who, What and Where. And always start with Who? We can't have drama without people. Then make sure that the What contains an issue or a problem of some kind. If the drama is to be dramatic you will need to put those people in a challenging situation, one which confronts them with difficult choices.

Most of the Extended Examples in Part 4 indicate some of the ways these dramas link with other curriculum areas.

3

Planning and assessment

Good planning should not be prescriptive and limiting; it should help you think the work through so that it is appropriate and beneficial for the particular children you're working with. It should also make you feel more secure as a teacher and give you greater flexibility.

This part is essentially concerned with how to think about planning. The Extended Examples in Part 4 show how this works in practice, with several of the examples teasing out the specifics of a planning process as well as looking at the practice itself.

Content

6
Planning and assessment

- Assessing relevant factors which affect planning
- Aims and objectives
- Dramatic starting points
- A lesson plan
- Assessment and evaluation

Embedded example:

- Personal evaluation of a drama lesson

Assessing relevant factors which affect planning

In planning any drama work – whether it is a single lesson or an extended cross-curricular project – we have to start by considering the factors we should take into account. What should affect our planning?

These factors can be summarised as follows:

- the children
- the teacher
- the curriculum
- other circumstances.

This order is significant. However prescribed a curriculum might be 'it is the children who are the learners . . . , and this gives them the key position . . . . The children must be allowed to do their own learning' (Fines and Verrier 1974: 17–18).

The children

- What are their interests?
- What are their strengths?
- What do you perceive their needs to be?
- How do they function as a group?
- What experience do the children have of drama, and of the lesson subject matter?

In drama we need to work with the interests of the children. That doesn't mean that if a large number of boys in the class are interested in motor bikes, and our topic is Roman Britain, we should put the legion in crash helmets. But we do need to observe the children we are working with closely and perceptively. What is likely to hold their interest in this project? Divided loyalties? Conquest? Betrayal? Bullying? A drama project about Roman Britain could deal with any of those.

What do they need? Maybe they are a group with no experience of compromise. Then in your planning you might focus on the need for negotiation and making concessions. In the process, you would be directly addressing the National Curriculum PSHE and citizenship objectives concerning 'Developing good relationships and respecting the differences between people'.

Maybe they are a group with poor command of spoken English, maybe some of the children desperately need to develop confidence in their writing skills. Then we bear this in mind and we try to structure the drama to meet some of those needs. Our knowledge of the children and the social health of the group informs and colours all subsequent thinking. The better we know the children, the more finely tuned we can make our starting point.

The teacher

At the centre of all teaching is the teacher/pupil relationship. It is misguided to ignore half of the equation. We should stand back and assess ourselves. How can we make the most of our strengths, develop our own skills? As a teacher you have to know your own comfort level. While it is good to take risks, they should be measured. We need to extend ourselves, but not always be working at the limits of our ability. If you feel uncomfortable working in role, for example, structure the lesson and scheme of work to give yourself the opportunity to try it out, to develop your skills, but don't lumber yourself with leading the whole session through role until you feel confident about it as a strategy.

If you can see the potential of using the whole group strategy, but are worried that it seems complicated, plan for small group activities that lead up to a short period of whole group work towards the end of the session.

The curriculum

We have to deliver a curriculum. We owe it to our children to do so. But we should never lose sight of the fact that the real 'consumers' in education are the children; the curriculum should be for the benefit of the children, not the other way round. You will find some drama books which propose setting out your objectives from the National Curriculum and the Primary Framework and then planning your schemes of work and lessons around delivering these objectives. The problem with this is that it is likely to *limit* the learning, not focus it. I would argue that it is much more productive to see your planning in drama as a way of creating *possible learning opportunities*. You should give careful consideration to the kind of learning opportunities the drama will offer; but the drama and the children's learning will suffer if you plan to meet specific targets. This is not to argue that you should abandon aims and objectives; you do, of course, need to have a clear sense of purpose and direction when you start, but your aims and objectives should be framed around the content of the drama itself.

The key to planning good drama is not having a million and one ideas, or in ticking off targets achieved, but in seeking dramatic situations which are likely to engage the children and develop their thinking; situations which contain the seeds of difficult dilemmas; situations which the children can relate to; which encourage them to think about the world they live in; which empower them as human beings. When they are wholeheartedly engaged in doing this, you will find the whole curriculum greatly enriched.

It is, however, worth identifying in advance *possible* links with the National Curriculum and Primary Framework. This is the approach I have adopted in the Extended Examples, where possible links are noted. In practice, most of these dramas were taught several times, with different groups of children in different ways. If you use and adapt any of these examples, you should be alert throughout to the specific learning opportunities that arise with your class and the learning that is actually taking place.

Other circumstances

These range from down-to-earth practical considerations to important long-term educational goals.

- Where is the drama to be taught?
- How long do you have in the space?
- To what extent can you support the drama work with research and related work in other curriculum areas?
- How might the drama feed into other curriculum work?
- Can you collaborate with any other teachers?
- Can you involve any other adults in the work?

Aims and objectives

There are several different ways of looking at aims and objectives. Perhaps the simplest is to think of aims as being long term and guiding. They should point us in a particular direction and they should allow for flexibility. The achievement of an objective, however, can be measured. In our objectives we can state that 'By the end of the lesson or project, the children will have done x, y and z.' And in some cases we'll have achieved it, in others not. The fact that sometimes we don't achieve all our objectives (perhaps because other more immediate learning opportunities have presented themselves) does not mean we're bad teachers. We need aims and objectives, but we also need flexibility. Good planning caters for that flexibility.

Consider the analogy of going down to the shops to buy a block of ice cream. Your aim is to have ice cream with fruit for Sunday lunch. Your objective is to go to the corner shop a couple of blocks away, where they sell ice cream. If, on the way you find there's an ice-cream van parked, you don't need to go to the shop. Your objective is a way of achieving your aim, and objectives can and will change during the course of a scheme of work.

Redundant aims

Aims and objectives such as 'to encourage co-operation', 'to develop sensitivity to others' may well be worthy in themselves, but there is no point including them in a specific scheme of work because we can assume that they guide and underpin *all* the drama that we do in the school. Aims may not be easy to formulate, but it is well worthwhile making the effort; they should always be specific.

Another type of aim that frequently appears in schemes of work for drama:

- 'The children should enjoy the drama'; or that
- 'First and foremost the drama should be fun.'

Of course learning should be enjoyable; but the worrying implication of the 'drama for enjoyment' type of aim is that other subject areas aren't. A good teacher should always make the subject interesting. The hard fact is that drama is not always going to be enjoyable in a superficial way; it should *not* always be fun; there are times when it should be difficult.

'Lost treasure' (described in Chapter 3), 'The Deserter' (Chapters 12) and 'The Coming of the Railway' (Chapter 13) all involve confronting and exploring the consequences of 'bad decisions'. Some of this exploration was difficult for the teachers and the children; but learning which shifts perceptions is often not easy. Presuming that all children want from life is 'good fun' is patronising and undervalues children.

Any drama scheme should include aims which fall into the following categories:

- *Content*
  Those aims which relate to the content of the work. What's the project going to be about, what's it going to be exploring?

- *Dramatic form*
  Those aims which relate to drama as an art form. What are the children going to learn about the art form of drama? What do you hope to teach them about drama itself?

■ *Social*

Those aims which relate to the children's social health – ranging, for example, from getting boys and girls to work collaboratively in small groups to 'resolving differences by looking at alternatives . . .'.

Dramatic starting points

How to start? As a simple principle, it is useful to begin by opening up your thinking about any given topic: try to think laterally, give yourself breadth so that you can then start focusing in on the specific. Having assessed the preconditions and considered what the children want to do, what you feel they need to do and how it might relate to the curriculum, you're ready to start looking for an appropriate *dramatic starting point*; the point where the drama itself really gets going.

The dramatic starting point may not be where the first lesson of a scheme begins. You may need to do some preliminary work to prepare the children (and possibly yourself) for the 'meat' of the drama. In whole group drama the dramatic starting point will frequently be the moment when the teacher enters in role. Here, for example are what we might term the dramatic starting points of some of the projects documented elsewhere in the book:

■ 'The Giant Awakes' (Chapter 5) – the Mayor calls a meeting of the townspeople to assess what they should do about the damage.

■ *Children's Games* (Chapter 9) – townsperson addressing a meeting, suggesting they escape poverty by emigrating.

■ 'The Deserter' (Chapter 12) seeks sanctuary in the village.

■ 'The Coming of the Railway' (Chapter 13) surveyor asks for labourers to help in drawing up a route map. This poses a threat to the community; it will have to cope with change.

In each of these examples the dramatic starting point creates dramatic tension; it poses a dilemma and asks the children to make a decision in role. In each case, the children were engaged in preliminary activities which led to the dramatic starting point; preliminary work which included research, role play, writing and exercises. There will be other times when you want to jump in at the deep end, as it were, and start with the dramatic starting point. Wherever you use it, however, it should be strong and engaging, containing at least the seeds of a dilemma.

In order to find an appropriate starting point, it is often useful to go through a series of simple tasks:

Brainstorming

Setting down as visually as possible any and every idea that comes into your head on the topic. It is important not to censor yourself as you do this. You may well find yourself going off at a tangent; you may well find that you come up with ideas that are inappropriate for the age group. Follow them through – almost like doing a word association game, but set it down visually. The process is itself liberating and opens up new possibilities.

Groups of people

Then ask yourself about the people involved. Simply list all the groups of people referred to or implicated in some way.

Possible dramatic frames

While you're still trying to think broadly about the topic, begin to consider the various dramatic frames. Is the drama set in the here and now, moving forwards as a simple linear narrative? Are we in the future, looking backwards at the present? From whose point of view do we see the events of the drama? Could it work as an investigation or an enquiry?

Finding a dramatic starting point

You should now have a variety of ways of looking at the topic. This is the point at which you need to start focusing these ideas down, seeking out a dramatic situation involving one of the groups of people you've listed; preferably a situation which contains a dilemma of some kind.

The key organising question

As discussed in Chapter 3, it is useful to formulate one of your aims as a question. What are we trying to find out through the drama? This should be a question to which the teacher does not know the answer. A well chosen Key Organising Question makes it easier to keep the drama focused, and will itself sometimes lead you to appropriate activities. For example, 'How can anyone ever leave the Old World completely behind?' (*The Arrival*) 'How can we confront and overcome our fears when others mock us?' (*The Tunnel*) Even if we can't answer the question, the drama will at least help us to respond to it.

Structure and organisation

- How do you prepare for the dramatic starting point?
- How do you introduce it?
- Are you using the teacher in role strategy? If so, how?
- What materials will you / the children need?
- What preparations need to be made in the drama space?

The organisation of the lesson will include noting all those preliminary activities which are sometimes needed to prepare the children for the work ahead. But the preparation time should not be used as a way of avoiding the drama; that's where the real learning takes place.

A lesson plan

Schools and colleges have their own way of setting out lessons plans. The following is offered as a way of revealing the thinking that might go into developing a lesson plan for some of the work suggested in Chapter 9, *Children's Games*. It should be seen as a guide, not a template.

Pre-conditions

Class: Year 4

Space and Time available: School Hall 1.30–2.30 pm

Classroom then available for immediate follow up work 2.30 to 3.15.

Other relevant factors affecting planning decisions

The school is an inner-city multi-racial school in the middle of Reading. Approximately half the children are white, the other half contains a wide range of ethnic groups. Although this is a one-off lesson, the children have some previous experience of drama with last year's teacher. There is an even mix of boys and girls in the class. The class have been studying Tudors in history. This lesson is likely to be the first in a project lasting about three weeks. Two further drama sessions are available at the same time.

Rationale

Many of the children (both boys and girls) enjoy various forms of science fiction on television, the cinema and in the books they choose to read. They are familiar with the concept of time travelling through films.

Aims

Content

- to explore the passing of time, and thereby familiarise the children with preliminary notions of history;
- to explore the effect of economic circumstances on people in Tudor times;
- to develop skills of deductive reasoning.

Key organising question

- How do we show people whose culture is very different from our own that we are peaceful?

Formal

- to introduce the concept of 'still images' as a narrative device in drama;
- to develop the sense of an appropriate vocal register;
- to encourage the children who have English as a second language to use their own first language within the fiction of the drama;
- to develop the children's questioning skills.

Social

- to encourage the boys and girls to work together in small groups;

Objectives

The children will:

- 'hot seat' and question the teacher and use powers of deductive reasoning to decide on courses of action;
- develop research skills and then use their findings to inform the drama;
- work together in small groups collaboratively, creating still images and then interpreting the work of others in a dramatic context.

Opportunities will be created for members of the class for whom English is a second language to use their own first language in role as part of the drama.

For relevant National Curriculum and Primary Framework links and possible learning opportunities see pp. 177–80.

Introductory activities

1. Control exercises:

   a) listening to the fading sound of Indian bells;

   b) using Indian bells as a signal to 'freeze' movement.

2. Looking at individual children in 'frozen' positions. Suggesting titles or captions for these, as if they were still photographs.

3. Small group work: making still images as if they were photographs taken on a holiday.

4. Small group work: making still images based on extracts from *Children's Games* painting

In practice you would also need to consider carefully the amount of time you intended to spend on each of these introductory activities.

Dramatic starting point

Teacher in role as a historian who has no experience of using a time machine, wants to travel back in time to the village where Bruegel painted *Children's Games* to find out where all the adults were when the picture was painted, but knows time travel is very dangerous. Teacher seeking advice from children, in role as experienced time travellers who have been to the village and returned with 'hologram pictures'.

Likely activities from here on

- Time travellers (the children) teaching the historian the rules of time travel. What are the dangers? What precautions do we need to take to minimise the dangers?

- Time travellers questioning the historian (hot seating) to see if she is fit to travel in time. What qualities are they looking for? How can they be certain she is sufficiently responsible?

- Representing the Time Machine.

- Having travelled back in time to the village, the teacher (as historian) could act as Devil's Advocate, breaking the rules of time travel. What is to be done?

In subsequent lessons the focus may change to the problems and dilemmas of the community. If necessary the teacher or children could change roles.

Strategies and techniques likely to be used after the dramatic starting point has been reached

- still image making

- teacher in role

- writing in role

- unrehearsed small group work, leading to Forum Theatre and spotlighting

- small group improvisations prepared and presented to the class in the context of video evidence

- meetings.

Resources

1. Sugar paper, felt tip pens, Blu-Tack®, children's notebooks, pencils, chairs, PE mats.

2. Other items which will be useful if available: laptop, digital camera and data projector, audio recorders.

Possible future developments

- meeting the people from the village;

- changing roles;

- a chart of missions back in time;

- further back in time – to the Stone Age. Why did the Stone Age people paint on cave walls?

- a dangerous mission to rescue a colleague lost in time;

- a time travel mission to find the makers of the first clocks.

Reflection

It is vitally important to build periods of reflection into the work. In this instance that could well take place back in the classroom immediately after the lesson; but there are occasions when it needs to happen in the hall. Never skimp on reflection. It's when children are given opportunities to think about what they've been doing that the real learning takes place.

Assessment and evaluation

In any form of assessment, evaluation or appraisal, we need to consider both our own performance as teachers, and to evaluate the work of the children. In terms of the children's work we need to consider them as individuals and as a class. Try to note the development of relevant social skills and drama skills, such as readiness to take on roles, ability to sustain a role, ability to construct and interpret still images. Some of these skills will be those referred to in the Primary Framework; others, such as the ability to understand and manipulate meaning beyond the literal, the ability to make use of close observation of others, are not easy to assess in quantifiable terms. In such cases a short note about the quality of the response will be useful to you in planning future drama work and in offering detailed reflective feedback to the children. Several examples of such observations can be found in the Extended Examples below.

When evaluating work always start by considering what has been achieved. Be critical in a positive sense. Try to pick out the strengths in the children's work, and in your own. The children can only get better at what they are doing if they know what they are doing well. This underlines the need for periods of reflection when you can help them discover the meanings and significance of their work and encourage them to be self-evaluative.

When writing an evaluation of a drama lesson be as specific as possible. Always try to use the evaluation not just to look back at what you have done, but also to look forward. Where next?

Occasionally try to record and evaluate a drama lesson in detail. The exercise will enhance your own skills of evaluation. One simple but effective way of recording the lesson is to lay out the documentation thus, with a straight-forward account of what happened on the left hand side of the page, and detailed comment on the right. Where there is no need for a comment, don't make one. The following brief example is based on the lesson plan earlier in the chapter.

Example

Personal evaluation of a drama lesson

Content and timing	Comment
1.30 The children enter the hall noisily. Three minutes to settle.	Better to have started with a concentration exercise in the classroom, and quietened them down before moving to the hall.
1.33 Indian bells concentration exercise.	Effective – possibly because it calms me as much as it calms them.
1.37 Indian bells as a control device for making still images.	Good transition. Children very responsive.
1.50 Still images in small groups. 'Holiday snaps'.	It's taken too long to get here. I'm rushing now, and that results in unclear instructions. Perhaps it would have been useful to have asked them to bring holiday snaps with them and represent these (might have been a good way in to details from *Children's Games*).
2.00 Viewing the scenes.	Good to see all the groups at the same time. The feedback to the whole group is helpful at this stage – particularly the reference to eye contact.
2.05 Making still images of details from *Children's Games*.	Instructions clear this time. Activity seems appropriate for the group. Small groups co-operating well together. Only group X and Y have any problem integrating boys and girls. But most groups' depictions betray worryingly sexist attitudes. Need to tackle these through the drama.

4 Extended examples

This part is in effect a development of the previous chapter. It looks further at planning and contains seven extended practical examples with an indication of the age range for which the work is appropriate. You should find, however, that the ideas that underpin the work are easily adaptable and can be used throughout the primary age range. They are offered as a stimulus for your own work with children; not as model lessons to be taught off the shelf or along rigid tramlines. It's important to be flexible and responsive to the children you're working with, so use what is helpful and be ready to adapt.

Each project is prefaced by reference to possible links to the Primary Framework for Literacy and/or the National Curriculum. These are offered as an indication of the range of *some* of the learning opportunities provided by the projects and the ways in which drama can enhance, support and complement work in other curriculum areas. The projects were not, however, designed with a view to delivering these as targets; and you will find that, in practice, working this way with children enables them to achieve far more than the key objectives presented here.

The concept of a 'text' appears frequently in the Primary Framework for Literacy documentation. This is sometimes interpreted in a limited sense, meaning a piece of writing – there are numerous references within these examples to children working with written texts both as researchers and as writers – but 'text' also refers to visual texts and performance texts. The poem *The Whale* is obviously a text, but so too is

Bruegel's picture, *Children's Games*; and in The Keeper of the Keys, the game is rigorously examined and analysed as a kind of performance text.

Each of the different examples has a different emphasis. Whale Island, The Deserter and The Coming of the Railway are accounts of taught drama projects, each with a slightly different emphasis; *Cinderella*, *The Tunnel*, *Children's Games* and Keeper of the Keys offer a wide range of suggestions for work and each considers, in slightly different ways, how you might plan this kind of work.

Contents

7

Cinderella

Reception classes and Years 1–2

This example offers a number of ways in which you might use a well-known traditional story to initiate and to develop drama. Some of the material is suited to reception age children, and some more appropriate for older children.

As with most traditional stories, the *Cinderella* story has been told and retold in numerous different ways, in very different tones. One thing that all the versions have in common is that it deals with a broken family, with problems, jealousies and injustices between children living in the same family who have different parents. This could touch raw nerves for many children; but if the material is sensitively handled it has the potential to be empowering and beneficial.

POSSIBLE NATIONAL CURRICULUM LINKS

Primary Framework for Literacy

Year 1

Speaking

- Retell stories, ordering events using story language.

Group discussion and interaction

- Take turns to speak, listen to others' suggestions and talk about what they are going to do.

Drama

- Explore familiar themes and characters through improvisation and role play. ▶

- Act out their own and well-known stories, using voices for characters.

Understanding and interpreting texts

- Identify the main events and characters in stories, and find specific information in simple texts.
- Make predictions showing an understanding of ideas, events and characters.

Engaging with and responding to texts

- Visualise and comment on events, characters and ideas, making imaginative links to their own experiences.

Primary Framework for Literacy: Year 2 Narrative Unit 2 Traditional Stories

Speaking

- Tell real and imagined stories using the conventions of familiar story language.

Listening and responding

- Respond to presentations by describing characters, repeating some highlights and commenting constructively.

Drama

- Present part of traditional stories, their own stories or work from different parts of the curriculum for members of their own class.

Understanding and interpreting texts

- Give some reasons why things happen and or characters change.

PSHE & Citizenship KS1 National Curriculum

Developing good relationships and respecting the differences between people

- 4d   That family and friends should care for each other.
- 4e   That there are different types of teasing and bullying, that bullying is wrong, and how to get help to deal with bullying.

Related activities in other curriculum areas

can be found at the end of the project.

Enacting the story that we know

If you have never tried to use drama in school, then one of the safest and easiest ways of introducing it is to use a well-known story and ask the children to enact it as you read it. They take on roles and participate in the actions of the story. The problem with this is that, because it does not allow the children any active choices, it limits their creativity and denies them any sense of ownership and therefore any responsibility for the material. If, however, the focus shifts from *what* they do to *how* they do it, enactment can be a useful first stage towards more open and creative work. Instead of simply telling the children what to do, try encouraging them to make decisions about *how* to represent specific moments in the story, then dwell on and tease out the meanings of these moments.

Example

Cinderella was 'employed in the meanest work of the house'. She has to clean the floors, scrub the dishes, lay the fire. *How* does she do this housework?

It's important not to allow this to become a kind of test for the children to see how well they match up to your reading of the story. If, for example, children scowl while enacting scrubbing the floor, it's better to accept this and *use* it rather than to try to correct them. 'I've always wondered how can she do all this really hard work and still stay cheerful? Can you show me how she looks when she's very tired, but wants her stepmother to think she's being cheerful?'

From enactments to dramatic exchanges

In the simple enactments described above, even if all the children in the class are enacting the same moment from the story at the same time, they are effectively working alone. Dramatic exchanges involve two or more people. In order for drama to develop we need to search the story for moments involving interaction between characters, in which some kind of decision is made.

Examples

Some moments in *Cinderella* with potential for dramatic exchanges:

■ The stepmother telling Cinderella what housework has to be done.

■ The stepsisters discussing what they are going to wear at the ball.

■ Cinderella helping the sisters to get ready.

■ The sisters taunting Cinderella, saying a maid could never attend a ball.

■ Cinderella first meeting with her fairy godmother.

■ Cinderella greeting the stepsisters after the ball.

■ Stepsisters telling her about the beautiful 'stranger' they have seen at the ball.

■ Prince talking to the guards, asking where the beautiful girl has gone.

■ Stepsisters begging Cinderella for forgiveness.

Consider what each of the characters intends or *wants* from the given situation; and, if possible, make these conflict. Thus, in the first of the above Cinderella might be simply complying with her stepmother's unfair instructions, but it would be more interesting if there was a reason for the stepmother to pretend to be nice to Cinderella for once. Similarly, the exchange will be more dramatic if Cinderella has a good reason for not doing the housework at this time. If there is an element of persuasion in a scene, the content is likely to become more interesting.

These simple exchanges involving two or three people can be undertaken by small groups working at the same time, or in front of the class. If the latter, then it is often useful for the teacher to take on a role, and it can be empowering for the children if the teacher takes on the lower-status role – for example a child as the stepmother, teacher as Cinderella. Then, using the methods of Forum Theatre (see p. 60) ask the class to work collaboratively to 'construct' the characters before you and a volunteer act out their ideas.

■ *How* do they talk?

■ What kind of things do they say? What kind of language do they use?

■ How can I persuade my stepmum that I need some time off?

Dramatising alternative endings

This can be especially useful with stories that the children have not previously encountered, where the strategy stimulates curiosity about the text and encourages active listening and active reading – how do the children's endings to the story compare with the written ending? Even with a story as well known as *Cinderella*, children quickly understand that they can make the story their own by adapting it in this way.

Examples

Explore what might happen if Cinderella's fairy godmother does not appear.

- What does Cinderella do while the sisters and her stepmother are away?

Explore what might happen if the fairy godmother is no good at magic.

- How can Cinderella help her fairy godmother to get the magic working?

Stop at the point where the stepsisters have just left the house.

- How might Cinders get into the ball?
- What else might she do if she decides she doesn't want to go to the ball?

Stop when she has met the prince and has returned home. The sisters and stepmother have not yet got back and she is alone in the house with her father.

- Can she tell her father what has happened?

Associated characters and their stories

The next stage in developing the drama might be to think beyond a series of short scenes involving small groups of two or three people. How to populate a drama? In preparation for the drama, you might make a list of all the people who are in any way directly involved with the story – in this instance, Cinderella, her father, her stepmother, her stepsisters, her fairy godmother, the prince, the king and queen, other guests at the ball; or you might do this with the children. Note – this list does not include characters, such as talking mice, from the pantomime version of the story. Explore possible exchanges that are implied by the story, but aren't usually recounted in it.

Example

- Cinderella's father telling her he has met someone and is going to get married.
- Sisters choosing fabric for their dresses.
- Sisters persuading their mother to buy them expensive clothes for the ball.

Then make a list of all those 'minor' characters who might in some way be connected with the story, but aren't usually mentioned in it:

Examples

- Cinderella's friends from her 'earlier life', before she had to spend all her life doing housework;
- neighbours;
- traders at the market and shops where Cinderella has to buy provisions;
- Cinderella's teacher (allowing a rather anachronistic approach to the story);
- the prince's mother and father (the king and queen);
- the workers at the palace who have to prepare the ball;
- the guards at the palace.

Explore these minor characters through thought-tracking or forum theatre:

- A neighbour trying to find out from the stepmother (teacher in role) 'what were those people from the palace doing round at your house?'

Developing roles

A technique sometimes referred to as *role on the wall* (see also p. 61) could be useful here to develop complexity in each of the characters, and encourage children to consider the difference between inner thoughts and feelings and outward appearances.

Example

Take one of the sisters, think about the following:

- Name?
  Rosamond.

- Describe her appearance:
  Short, red faced.

- Words to describe the way she treats Cinderella:
  Mean, impatient, angry, rude.

- What does she think about Cinderella?
  She's jealous of her.

- What does she think about herself?
  She doesn't like herself.

The resulting image might look something like Figure 7.1.

Explore what might have happened before the story starts

Examples

- Cinderella living with her father after her mother has died and before he meets his second wife. ▶

- Creating a wider community around the house where Cinderella lives with her new family. How do other people in the community know and interact with the family?
- King and queen persuading a shy prince that he should attend a ball.
- The sisters interacting with each other and their mother before they have Cinderella to bully.
- Palace workers preparing for the ball – decorating, preparing food, etc.

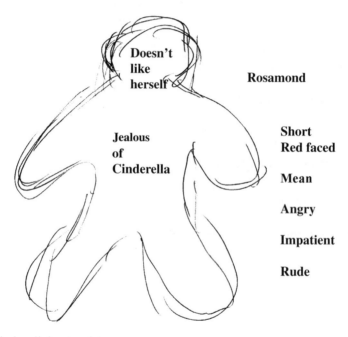

Figure 7.1 Cinderella's stepsister

Explore what's happening elsewhere while the well-known story is taking place

Examples

- Role play the setting of the story. Create a map of different areas (e.g. the village where Cinderella and her dad and stepfamily live, the market, shops, park) and explore in role.

- 'Fairy godmother' in disguise seeking directions from neighbours to find Cinderella's house.

- 'Fairy godmother' in disguise trying to borrow mice and rats from a pet shop and a pumpkin from a grocer – to transform.

- Fairy godmother as an incompetent magician, seeking the help of the children to get her magic to work her transformations.

Explore what happens after the known story has ended

Examples

- Can she persuade the prince to live with her and her father, rather than go and live in the palace?

- Neighbours try to persuade Cinderella to let them have a share of her new-found wealth.

- Class devises an 'education programme' to stop the sisters bullying anyone else.

- How does Cinderella deal with moving from being a scapegoat to having everything she wants? How does she like palace life?

Storyboarding: retelling the story through a sequence of still images

The children decide on those moments in the story that they think are the most important. Depending on the age, ability and experience of the children, this might be a task for small groups or for discussion between the teacher and the whole class. In small groups, the children then make *still images* of each of these moments. Once they have made the still images, the characters in each of the images could be developed through *thought tracking*. Dialogue could be added.

The images could be transferred to a class storyboard and/or comic strip. See note on Teaching Resources at the end of this chapter.

Retelling the story from a different point of view

In each of the following cases, the story can be dramatised using the methods described above. We might, for example, start by creating a sequence of five key still images, and then proceeding as in 'Storyboarding' above.

Examples

- Cinderella's father
- neighbours;
- the prince;
- the fairy godmother;
- the guards who see Cinderella leave, who accompany the prince as he seeks the girl who has left the glass slipper behind;
- Workers at the palace who have seen the ball.

Taking the story in a different direction

Examples

- Reporters try to get interviews with anybody who knows anything about the prince's new wife.
- Cinderella decides that she doesn't want to go to the ball.
- Cinderella asks the fairy godmother for an alternative to going to the ball.
- The prince is too shy to approach Cinderella without the advice and help of the children.

Related activities in other curriculum areas

Geography KS1 National Curriculum

Geographical enquiry and skills

2e   Make maps and plans

Mapping activities – places from the story: Prince Charming's Castle, Fairy Godmother's House, local village and features, surrounding environment (children to decide: near a forest, the sea?).

Music KS1 National Curriculum

Creating and developing musical ideas – composing skills

2b   Explore, choose and organise sounds and musical ideas, e.g. Soundscape for each of the places noted above.

Responding and reviewing – appraising skills

3a   Explore and express their ideas and feelings about music using movement, dance and expressive and musical language.

e.g. Selecting music for the Palace Ball. Listening to, discussing and responding to music.

Teaching resources

Websites

The Cinderella Project, based at University of Southern Mississippi, contains a text and image archive containing a dozen English versions of the fairy tale. http://www.usm.edu/english/fairytales/cinderella/cinderella.html

Sur La Lune Fairy Tales offers annotated versions of many traditional tales. The site includes histories, similar tales across cultures, modern interpretations and numerous illustrations. The *Cinderella* material can be found at: http://www.surlalunefairytales.com/cinderella/

A simple sequencing exercise, which relates to the storyboarding activity in the extended example, can be found on the educational website of the city of Birmingham (UK), *BGfL*, Birmingham Grid for Learning.
http://www.bgfl.org/bgfl/custom/resources_ftp/client_ftp/ks1/english/ story_telling/cinderella/cinderella1.htm

8
The Tunnel
Years 2–3

Based on the book by Anthony Browne, this example attempts to open up the thinking that underpins the planning for drama using a picture book story.

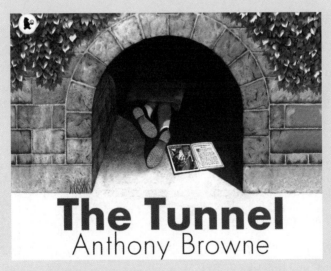

Figure 8.1 *The Tunnel* title page

POSSIBLE NATIONAL CURRICULUM LINKS

Primary Framework for Literacy

Narrative Unit 1 Stories with familiar settings

Year 2

Speaking

■ Sustain conversation, explain or give reasons for their views or choices.

Listening and responding

■ Respond to presentations by describing characters, repeating some highlights and commenting constructively.

Drama

■ Adopt appropriate roles in small or large groups and consider alternative courses of action.

■ Present part of traditional stories, their own stories or work drawn from different parts of the curriculum for members of their own class.

Understanding and interpreting texts

■ Give some reasons why things happen or characters change.

Engaging with and responding to texts

■ Engage with books through exploring and enacting interpretations.

Year 3

Speaking

■ Sustain conversation, explain or give reasons for their views or choices.

Listening and responding

■ Follow up others' points and show whether they agree or disagree in whole-class discussion.

Drama

■ Use some drama strategies to explore stories or issues.

Engaging with and responding to texts

■ Identify features that writers use to provoke readers' reactions.

National Curriculum PSHE & Citizenship

KS1

Preparing to play an active role as citizens

- 2a to take part in discussions with one other person and the whole class. Developing good relationships and respecting the differences between people.
- 4a to recognise how their behaviour affects other people.
- 4d that family and friends should care for each other.

KS2

Preparing to play an active role as citizens

- 2f to resolve differences by looking at alternatives, making decisions and explaining choices.
- 4a that their actions affect themselves and others, to care about other people's feelings and to try to see things from their points of view.

About the book

The Tunnel is a story about an unnamed brother and sister who are constantly quarrelling. She is nervous, interested in books; he likes playing outside with friends, 'laughing and shouting, throwing and kicking, roughing and tumbling'. She is afraid of the dark and he sometimes creeps into her room at night 'to frighten her'. One day their mother gets fed up of the fighting and bickering around the house and insists that they go out to play together. When his sister accompanies him to some waste ground, he moans that she's 'frightened of everything' and then goes off to explore on his own, finds a strange tunnel and, in spite of his sister telling him he shouldn't, he crawls down the tunnel. After waiting and waiting for him to come back, she follows him into the tunnel, which is even more scary than she had feared. She eventually emerges at the other end in a wood, filled with trees that seem to embody her worst fears – wolves, wild boars, an empty wicker basket, an axe lying beside a tree stump. She runs and runs until she gets through the wood – only to find her brother 'still as stone'. 'She threw her arms around the cold hard form . . .' and slowly he not only comes back to life but is grateful to her for having come after him.

As with all Anthony Browne's work, this kind of narrative summary merely scratches the surface of a book in which the details of the individual pictures are as intriguing and stimulating as the narrative. When the boy creeps into his sister's room to frighten her at night we see that she is fascinated by *Little Red Riding Hood*: a red cape hangs on the side of the wardrobe, a picture of Little Red meeting the wolf is fixed to the wall behind her bed, her bedside light is in the shape of a thatched cottage.

Figure 8.2 *The Tunnel*, the girl's bedroom

Figure 8.3 *The Tunnel*, the wild wood

When she gets through the tunnel and finds herself in the forest on the other side, these are the very things that threaten her. The trees have taken on the form of her nightmare.

Like *Red Riding Hood*, *The Tunnel*, is about growing up. Little Red gains independence and confronts her fears. In *The Tunnel* the girl has to face up to her fears, then overcomes them and gains self-esteem; instead of 'staying inside on her own' and being mocked by her brother, she becomes the sibling who takes action, she goes through the tunnel and rescues her brother. That is, however, one particular adult reading of the story. The reason for including the book here is to show how you might use drama to explore the range of meanings it might have for children.

Anthony Browne's stories and pictures provide a rich stimulus for discussion; children love the mixture of the familiar and the fantastic, the threatening and the homely, the mysterious and the real. My concern with a text as open and rich as this is to find ways of making the most of Anthony Browne's pictures and imagery, to make sure that I do not impose my own interpretation on the class, but, rather, to use drama itself to explore the question: 'I wonder what this story means?'

Drama

Pair work

The story offers some useful, straightforward starting points for pair work.

- brother and sister arguing;
- boy frightening his sister;
- mum ticking off the boy for frightening the sister;
- boy trying to persuade his sister to go with him through the tunnel.

The book contains useful snatches of dialogue that you might offer as a starting point, for example:

- 'Try to be nice to each other just for once.'
- 'Why did you have to come?'

There are, however, problems with this: the exchanges are likely to be limited and predictable – not least because, although the story ultimately challenges stereotypical gender roles, it starts by apparently confirming those roles.

In order for drama to develop – both in itself and in terms of understanding – we need to create situations with inherent tensions, not simply conflict; situations which contain the potential for change, for things to be other than the way they are (see 'Structure and dramatic tension' in Chapter 3). In the case of these short pair-work scenes, we need to create situations which do not simply degenerate into a slanging match. One practical way of doing this is to play out the scenes as Forum Theatre, with you, the teacher, taking on one of the roles. This enables you to play with the situation and add tension and possibilities for change where there might otherwise be an impasse. Forum Theatre also enables you to shift the gender roles and power within the relationship. You might, for example, play the boy while a girl from the class plays Mum ticking the boy off for frightening his sister; or play the girl and ask a quiet child to take on the role of the boy. Forum Theatre allows that person to ask for help – what should I say now? How should I say it?

Another way of developing the dramatic content of these simple pair-work improvisations is by reversing the roles, giving girls the opportunity to play the boy and vice versa. You may well encounter some initial resistance to this, but if tackled through forum, in which you can lead by example and ask the whole class *how* you should each play the role, what kind of things you should say, you are likely to find that many children do want to take on opposite gender roles, even though they need permission (usually in the form of active encouragement!) to do so.

The relationship at the heart of Anthony Browne's story is deliberately sketchy. All we know is that the brother and sister are 'different' and that they fight and argue. By adding certain constraints in the form of additional information – something you can do collaboratively with the children – it's possible to introduce tension and move the scenes beyond mere conflict. Each of the following suggestions modifies the scene in order to allow for the possibility of negotiation. At the beginning of the story, the girl seems to be dominated by her brother, but it's important not to allow the girls in the class to become alienated, so in most of the following examples the constraints take some of the power away from the boy:

Examples

Basic situation	Possible constraints
Boy frightening his sister.	The boy has gone in to his sister's room because he has himself had a nightmare. Frightening her is a way of feeling better about himself. They'll both be in trouble if they wake their parent(s).
Brother and sister arguing.	He wants her to help him with his homework.
Mum ticking off the boy for frightening the sister.	She wants him to apologise to her. He knows it wasn't his sister's fault that he was caught in her room, but he still blames her. Mum can use a sanction that will affect the boy (needs to be discussed in advance by the class).
Boy trying to persuade his sister to go with him through the tunnel.	He doesn't want to admit to her that he is as scared by the tunnel as he is excited by it.

Once children begin to understand how much more interesting the drama becomes when it moves beyond unresolved conflict, you can ask them for suggestions, then try them out. Ask what, for example, the brother and sister are arguing about – better to ask the girls in the class to state the boy's case, and the boys the girl's. You rapidly get to the point where the children themselves understand that the scene is more interesting if an argument is not simply a barrage of insults but instead can lead to some change of perspective. The pair-work scenes can then be played out in several different ways – so that the point of the work is exploration, not seeking a definitive version – and your job as teacher is to tease out meanings and potential for further development.

Further pair work by populating the drama beyond the story

Note that the mother herself is not illustrated in Anthony Browne's story and there is no mention of a father. Many children assume that the story is about a single-parent family, but when we use a story as a starting point there is no need to stick to the original – which should be seen as a stimulus, not a set of tram-lines. If we want to extend the frame of the drama by adding other characters, that might lead us to pair work such as:

- Mum and Dad worried about where the children have got to;
- Mum and/or Dad contacting the children's friends, relatives, neighbours, trying to find out where they might be.

And that in turn could lead us to whole group work – see below.

Focal point / the key organising question

If our prime aim with this material is to explore the question 'I wonder what this story means?', then secondary questions are likely to emerge during the pair work. If we want to take the work further, we need to give careful consideration to what we and the children want to explore in the story, what our focus or 'key organising question' is to be. When using this material with children, all of the following have emerged as central concerns in their responses to the dramatised story:

- being left out;
- bullying, being bullied, dealing with bullying;
- acknowledging, confronting and overcoming fears;
- loyalty;
- considering other people's feelings.

From a teacher's point of view, the story also provides opportunities to focus on:

- making plans;
- explaining, persuading, describing.

The focus, the key question, is what guides you both in your response to the children's work and in the way that you structure development. If, for example, you had chosen to focus on *acknowledging, confronting and overcoming fears,* you might use the last of the situations suggested above to raise the question, 'I wonder how difficult it is for a boy to allow his sister to rescue him.'

Throughout this, if the children (and probably the boys in particular) in your class are to take this seriously, you have to stress that your drama is about the 'imaginary boy' in *The Tunnel* drama, giving them permission to explore their own fears at a safe distance; using the protection of the role to allow them to play a frightened child. If this is your chosen focus, then your aim as a teacher might be to find and explore a situation where the boy in the story can admit his own fears, and seek help from his sister. You might then look for a technique to help you (collectively, i.e. you and the class) reach that point; something to enable the whole class to contribute to developing the role of the boy. There are many ways of doing this: one, using the techniques of Forum Theatre as already outlined; another might be to ask for a volunteer to take on the role of 'the boy' (who could easily be played by a girl) as he crawls through the tunnel. You then ask the rest of the class to make the tunnel using their own bodies, perhaps making two lines with arms outstretched and arching over.

Figure 8.4 *The Tunnel*, the tunnel entrance

As the volunteer walks or crawls through the tunnel each person can whisper what they think frightens the boy. Children's suggestions have ranged from the relatively simple and obvious to the profound and revealing: 'It's very dark', 'Spiders', 'Bats', 'You don't know what's at the other end', 'You'll never find your way back', 'You're alone.' This 'animated tunnel' is a form of the technique described elsewhere as *Conscience Alley*; and you might develop it by asking some children to voice (again in whispers to retain the atmospheric quality) the boy's determination to overcome his fears, with the children offering the teacher advice on how to deal with the worried child asking for help.

You may find that several children say similar things – it gets increasingly difficult to be original as 'the boy' approaches the end of the line – but your job here as teacher is to draw meaning from their suggestions, to work with what they give you. If several children say 'it's so dark', then pick up on that and use it as if it is the thought process of the boy himself. When *reflecting* on work, it is always better to draw meaning from what the children have done rather than suggesting what else they might have done. In this instance you might say something along the lines of: 'The darkness is really troubling for him, isn't it? I'm not surprised. When we're frightened or worried, things go round and round in our head, don't they?'

The process itself begins to open up one of the most important aspects of the drama which, expressed rather grandly, we might call putting us in touch with our common humanity: it enables us to see that we often share hopes and that we are not alone in suffering from our fears and anxieties.

On a practical level, you might also build up a soundscape for the boy's journey through the tunnel, with the children who are making the tunnel walls also contributing sounds, such as dripping water. You might also add atmospheric music – either pre-recorded or music that the children themselves make using instruments. Thus the journey itself takes on significance, and you encourage the children to feel part of something exciting in itself.

Note that in all this work we are expanding the story, and by doing so stimulating imaginative responses to it. In Anthony Browne's original story, the boy is turned to stone – a powerful metaphor, which you might explore with the children – but the key dramatic moment in the story is when his sister rescues him. If the drama work has to be confined to the classroom, you might well take the girl through the animated tunnel and then use Forum Theatre again, to develop the 'rescue' itself, by asking questions such as:

- What has happened to the boy that he finds himself unable to move?
- How does he communicate that he's pleased to see his sister?

In any Forum Theatre work, where the issues or situation is potentially raw, leaving a child open to mockery from their peers, you can offer to take on the role yourself, and create a specific problem or task which you have to solve *with the help of the class*. Thus, in this instance, you might take on the role of the boy 'turned to stone'. In the case of one class I worked with on this project he had become so frightened by this strange place that he couldn't move; and his 'problem' was that in order to be rescued by his sister he had to admit to her that he was frightened.

Whole group work

Although Forum Theatre and the 'animated tunnel' exercise do involve the whole class, it is not whole group drama in that the focus is always on one or two people. To develop the story as a whole group you might move on from the point at which the boy has gone through the tunnel and, taking on the role of the girl, go to the class and seek their help to go in search of her lost brother. This then becomes a group expedition with group responsibilities. They will need to make careful plans: what do they need to take with them? And how do they deal with their own fears about going through the tunnel? As the drama develops you (collectively) may want to populate the world on the other side of the tunnel, creating and tackling new problems, posing and responding to new questions.

Other, related activities

The following could be incorporated into the above, but they are also worth-while self-contained activities in themselves:

- *Change the story* so that after the boy has disappeared through the tunnel, the girl does not immediately follow him, but is worried by his disappearance and is feeling guilty because she thinks it is her fault. Using the medium of Forum Theatre again, and with the teacher taking on the role of the girl, explore how her Mum might encourage her to explain what has happened.
- *Blind exercise* – child leads either the teacher or another child through the environment at the other end of the tunnel.
- *Descriptions* of bedroom, waste ground, the tunnel, what's on the other side of the tunnel.
- *Give directions* that will enable people to find the strange piece of waste ground where they found the tunnel.
- Make *emotional maps* (see pp. 123–4) of the environment around the family home. How does this emotional map change after the girl has rescued her brother?

Teaching resources

Many of Anthony Browne's picture books for young children are excellent resources for use with children throughout the primary school, and lend themselves to the kind of work described in this extended example.

In *Pupils as Playwrights* (Woolland 2008: 85–9) there is a case study based on work on Anthony Browne's *Voices in the Park*.

9
Children's Games
Years 3–4

This example focuses on the painting *Children's Games* by Pieter Bruegel. The methodology employed exemplifies the ways you might use an image as a stimulus for drama; and also some of the ways in which skills of observation can be developed and linked to imaginative speculation.

POSSIBLE NATIONAL CURRICULUM LINKS

Primary Framework for Literacy

Year 4 Narrative – Unit 1 Stories with historical settings

1998 Framework objectives covered

- Year 4, Term 1: T1 building character and setting from details; T2 identify main characteristics and predict actions.

KS2 History

Unit 8: What were the differences between the lives of rich and poor people in Tudor times?

- Children learn about the lives of different types of people living in Tudor times. Children will find out about the characteristic features of society at a time in the distant past by asking and answering questions from a range of different sources of information.

▶

KS 2 Art

Unit 3A: Portraying relationships

■ Children investigate how paintings, prints, photographs and other images that include figures communicate ideas about relationships.

PSHE & Citizenship KS2 National Curriculum

Preparing to play an active role as citizens

■ 2e to reflect on spiritual, moral, social and cultural issues, using imagination to understand other people's experiences.

■ 2f to resolve differences by looking at alternatives, making decisions and explaining choices.

■ 2j that resources can be allocated in different ways and that these economic choices affect individuals, communities and the sustainability of the environment.

Developing good relationships and respecting the differences between people

■ 4b to think about the lives of people living in other places and times, and people with different values and customs.

The painting

There are many ways of using a painting or photograph as a starting point for drama. Whenever you embark on planning a drama, however, you need to ask yourself similar questions. These can be summarised as:

■ *Who* is involved?
■ *What* has happened up to now?
■ *When* and *Where* is the drama taking place?
■ What is the inherent problem in the situation that creates dramatic tension?

The following suggestions for small group work are a way of using a painting as a stimulus to develop initial ideas for a drama, to give children opportunities to address these questions directly themselves. These are followed by brief suggestions for using the painting as a starting point for whole group drama.

Figure 9.1 *Children's Games* (*Kinderspiele*) by Pieter Bruegal the Elder

You might start by asking the children to look closely at the whole painting and see if they recognise any of the games being played. There are more than 200 children represented in the painting and it is said that at least 80 different 'games' have been identified. These include many different kinds of games: some are potentially rough (the blindfold game discussed below, the blind see-saw on a barrel), some are reckless and perhaps involve a dare (disturbing a beehive) or bullying (hair pulling); some are team games (tug o' war on 'horseback') while others are solitary (the girl with her doll); some demand physical dexterity (jacks) while others require mental skills (playing cards). Also, appropriately in this context, where we are using painting for drama, we see role play (a wedding game and 'horse racing' on the wooden fence).

Small group work

We might start by interrogating a particular image extracted from the painting (Figure 9.2).

Essentially, we are asking the children to look carefully at the extract from the painting and think about facial expression, body language and positioning, to

Figure 9.2 Blindfold games

develop an imaginative response to the painting based on close observation; but it's a useful principle to start with description, and then move on to interpretation: i.e. this is what we see in the picture, and then, this is what we understand it to mean.

The focus of this extract is a blindfold game of some kind. If we ignore the child in the background leaning against the fence, there are seven children in this section of the picture. Two are blindfold and the game seems to be a kind of Blind Man's Buff in which one child is being led away from another who is reaching out, but not actually in contact with anybody. Although the expressions are only sketched it seems that the boy on the right of the painting, holding his hand to his mouth, looks worried. Two other children are looking round the wall of a building.

They seem to be excited by the game, but not part of it. A smaller child, an enigmatic figure, has his/her back to us and is bending slightly forwards. It's not clear whether s/he is blindfolded or is simply wearing a scarf of some kind. The picture which seems relatively simple offers various opportunities for opening up discussion about feelings – to talk about, for example, what might be worrying the boy with the hand up to his mouth, and whether the two children peeping round the wall are feeling left out.

Ideally, it would be good to develop this account of the picture in collaboration and discussion with the children – either by projecting the image or by photocopying it.

The next task can either be undertaken by a single group in front of the class, or by dividing the class into small groups. You would need to be confident about the social health of the class for them to work relatively independently in (say) four groups of seven. Your discussion of the picture could be limited to body language and positions and facial expression, or it might include talking about costumes and historical context. The depth of the discussion depends on the ability and experience of the children. For an inexperienced class, your focus is likely to be initially on the 'game' itself; for a class used to working in this way you might quickly move to thinking about the historical context.

- In groups create a still image of the people from the painting. What might the people in this image be saying? What might they feel about each other? Add dialogue, add thoughts, add a caption. Bring it to life.

- Think about this same group of people, and talk about what each of them might have been doing five minutes before. What led up to this moment? Create another image to show this.

- Repeat for a few hours earlier in the day.

- Still focusing on the same group of people, but instead of moving backwards in time, go forwards – initially, say, five minutes and then to the end of the day.

These simple tasks lead to a 'storyboard' of five still images, with the middle image being the 'now' of the detail from the painting, with short dialogue, thoughts and captions; developing storytelling and particularly the understanding of cause and effect narrative. The storyboard, storytelling exercise could in turn lead you back to art work, with children creating their own pictures in the style of Bruegel, and using a similar colour palette.

Whole group work

To develop whole group drama from this starting point we need to give more attention to the *when* and *where* questions, and to decide on an inherent problem in the situation that will create dramatic tension. This may well emerge from the work on still images, but it would also be worth returning to the whole painting and, if they have not already noticed it themselves, drawing attention to other aspects of the painting. You might, for example, wonder why Bruegel chose to make the building which looks as if it might be the town hall so important; to wonder 'Why are there no adults to be seen?'

One class I worked with on this material used the storyboards as a way of building up a sense of a small urban community in Tudor England, relating the drama to their work in History on the differences between the lives of rich and poor people in Tudor times; moving quickly from the initial focus on the children's games to the adults' work in the town. Here are some suggestions for possible starting points, all of which allow the children to incorporate the ideas they have worked on in making their storyboards into the context of a larger dramatic fiction.

- The class take on roles as the people depicted in the painting, but twenty years forward in time. Now in role as adults, they are asked to recollect what was happening in their lives when Bruegel came to their town and painted the picture. Possible roles for teacher: investigator, map maker, census officer.

- The teacher in role as Bruegel. 'I visited this town twenty years ago and I was paid to paint this picture. And now, at last, I am able to return and give it to you. But things have changed so much. What has happened in the meantime?'

- Our drama could use the qualities of strangeness in the painting, trying to answer the question 'Why are / were there so few adults in it?' 'Where were they when the painter was here?' In the case of the class referred to above, they decided that the children were playing alone because the adults had to work so hard. I then asked the children to take on the roles of the adults in this community, which we then developed using the principles and methods described in Chapter 2 (pp. 51–4).

In each of these suggestions, however, although the teacher and the children have a role, there is not yet a specific problem to focus the drama. In my experience, children will themselves introduce all manner of issues – they like things to be dramatic – but in order to use their ideas productively, you do need to be confident of your own ability to respond quickly to such suggestions, to give them a clear focus, and to be working in a school environment where such flexibility is possible.

Many drama teachers working on whole group drama often start by using a role to bring a problem to the drama. Each of the following three suggestions would enable you to start in this way. (This methodology is a characteristic of Process Drama. Several books recommended in the Resources section are devoted to this method of working.) In each instance I have made the assumption that the class, taking on the roles of the adults who are missing from Bruegel's picture, have gathered for a meeting of some kind and that they are familiar with the teacher taking on a role in the drama.

1. 'I understand that the children have been sent outside to play. Thank you for that. It is best that they don't hear what we have to discuss. It is that time of year again. We have to pay tithes. I cannot afford to pay; and I know that many of my neighbours are in the same position. We have nothing. Our harvest has been dreadful.'

    The focus of the drama here could be on how the poor might share the burden of paying tithes between them. Although this creates a problem for the townspeople, it does not of itself create the kind of tension that can make drama so productive and exciting (see pp. 76–8). For that we need a dilemma, in which children can clearly see pros and cons; which allows them to take up a position and then explore the consequences of their attitudes and their decisions. An example in this instance might be for the person addressing the meeting (the teacher in role) to suggest they escape poverty by emigrating.

If this is to be historically accurate, however, it demands that we shift the setting for the drama to a later period in European history, say 1860.

2. 'You have asked me to go to the Manor House and request that because the harvest has been so dreadful this year we be relieved from paying our tithes. You have asked me because I am the oldest person here; and I am willing to go. But I don't know what to say. I need accurate written information about the situation we are in; and I need your help in writing letters, making maps to show how we live and how little food we have.'

   If the focus of this drama is on the National Curriculum History Unit 8 (*What were the differences between the lives of rich and poor people in Tudor times?*), you might ask the class to change roles, so that in due course they take on the role of those collecting the tithes.

3. 'Fellow astronauts, we are about to travel back in time to visit our own planet, Planet Earth, in the year 1560. We shall arrive at a small town. You have been chosen for this mission because of your expertise. We need to be sure that we blend in with the people of this village. How should we dress? How should we prepare ourselves to go amongst them? . . . Remember, we are working for the Museum of Earth History and our task is to find out as much as possible about their way of life and to bring back holograms of daily life in this town.'

   In this drama, the still images the children had created could now be placed in a developing fictional context, taking on the status of reconstructions or holograms for the Museum.

The dramas in 2 and 3 above would demand a great deal of cross-curricular work. A detailed account of a developed whole group drama can be found in the extended example 'The Coming of the Railway'. Although this is aimed at children in Years 5 and 6, the principles – creating dilemmas, allowing children genuine choice, exploring the consequences of the decisions they make – can be applied productively to any of the suggestions above.

Although Bruegel probably painted *Children's Games* at around 1560 and it depicts some of the games played by the children of Flemish peasants, many of the games are still played. The painting lends itself to being used as part of a historical project, but if you focus on the games themselves and the body language and facial expressions of the children, it can easily be used as a starting point for drama set in different times: for example, evacuees during the Second World War.

Three further details extracted from *Children's Games* which could be useful for developing drama in this way are reproduced below:

Figure 9.3 Girl and her doll (a); horse racing role play (b); and playing jacks (c)

Teaching resources

Although not all Pieter Bruegel's paintings are suitable for use with children in the primary school, many of them are rich in detail and give a fascinating insight into medieval life. They offer rich stimuli for starting drama work, and for historical research. Look particularly at: *The Hunters in the Snow*, *Peasant Wedding*, *The Peasant Dance*, *The Tower of Babel* and *Hay Making*. Several books of reproductions are available. The following is recommended as a good cheap paperback edition for children: *The Life & Work of Pieter Bruegel* by Jayne Woodhouse, Heinemann, 2001.

Websites

Pieter Bruegel's *Kinderspiele* is held at the Kunsthistorisches Museum Vienna, website: http://www.khm.at/homeE/homeE.html

Downloadable reproductions of the painting, including detailed enlargements from it, can be found at:
http://bilddatenbank.khm.at/viewArtefact?id=321&image=GG_1017_HP.jpg

The Web Gallery of Art also has downloadable reproductions of *Children's Games* (including excellent details) and many other Bruegel paintings.
http://www.wga.hu/frames-e.html?/html/b/bruegel/pieter_e/painting/children/index.html

The Arty Factory website is highly recommended for older children. The page about *Children's Games* and perspective includes a short, but excellent and stimulating commentary on the picture.
http://www.artyfactory.com/perspective_drawing/perspective_14.htm

10
Keeper of the Keys
Years 3–6

The prime purpose of this chapter is to look at how it is possible to use a dramatic game to explore meanings beyond the literal through playful, interactive explorations of metaphor and symbolism.

The example also illustrates how one might use a game to:

- create a 'back story' as a basis for drama; and as a stimulus for storytelling and creative writing;
- demonstrate how to manipulate dramatic tension;
- encourage and develop listening skills;
- develop roles and narrative within a game and expand them into a drama;
- develop scripts from improvised drama.

The essence of the methodology proposed here is to seek out those elements in the game which imply some kind of role play (inherent in many games, even in the simplest 'tag'), to use this to develop a narrative, and explore dramatic situations within that narrative.

POSSIBLE NATIONAL CURRICULUM LINKS

Primary Framework for Literacy

Year 3

Speaking

- Sustain conversation, explain or give reasons for their views or choices.
- Develop and use specific vocabulary in different contexts.

▶

Listening and responding

■ Follow up others' points and show whether they agree or disagree in whole class discussion.

Group discussion and interaction

■ Use talk to organise roles and action.
■ Actively include and respond to all members of the group.
■ Use the language of possibility to investigate and reflect on feelings, behaviour or relationships.

Drama

■ Present events and characters through dialogue to engage the interest of an audience.
■ Use some drama strategies to explore stories or issues.

Understanding and interpreting texts

(Note: in this instance, the game itself is being used as a text, which is then read and subjected to detailed and rigorous analysis.)

■ Infer characters' feelings in fiction and consequences in logical explanations.
■ Identify how different texts are organised.
■ Use syntax, context and word structure to build their store of vocabulary as they read for meaning.

Engaging with and responding to texts

■ Empathise with characters and debate moral dilemmas portrayed in texts.

Text structure and organisation

■ Signal sequence, place and time to give coherence.

Year 4

Speaking

■ Offer reasons and evidence for their views, considering alternative opinions.

- Respond appropriately to the contributions of others in the light of differing viewpoints.
- Tell stories effectively and convey detailed information coherently for listeners.

Listening and responding

- Listen to a speaker, make notes on the talk and use notes to develop a role play.

Group discussion and interaction

- Take different roles in groups and use the language appropriate to them, including the roles of leader, reporter, scribe and mentor.

Drama

- Create roles showing how behaviour can be interpreted from different viewpoints.
- Develop scripts based on improvisation.

Engaging and responding to texts

- Interrogate texts to deepen and clarify understanding and response.

Creating and shaping texts

- Use settings and characterisation to engage readers' interest.
- Show imagination through the language used to create emphasis, humour, atmosphere or suspense.
- Choose and combine words, images and other features for particular effects.

Year 5

Speaking

- Present a spoken argument, sequencing points logically, defending views with evidence and making use of persuasive language.

Listening and responding

- Identify some aspects of talk that vary between formal and informal occasions.

▶

Group discussion and interaction

- Understand the process of decision making.

Drama

- Reflect on how working in role helps to explore complex issues.
- Perform a scripted scene making use of dramatic conventions.
- Use and recognise the impact of theatrical effects in drama.

Engaging and responding to texts

- Compare the usefulness of techniques such as visualisation, prediction and empathy in exploring the meaning of texts.

Year 6

Speaking

- Use a range of oral techniques to present persuasive arguments and engaging narratives.
- Use the techniques of dialogic talk to explore ideas, topics or issues.

Listening and responding

- Listen for language variation in formal and informal contexts.

Drama

- Improvise using a range of drama strategies and conventions to explore themes such as hopes, fears and desires.

Creating and shaping texts

- Integrate words, images and sounds imaginatively for different purposes.

Description of the game

Keeper of the Keys is sometimes known as Hunter and Hunted. There are many versions; and, as with any game, the rules can be changed or adapted to suit the participants.

Children all sit in a circle. Two volunteers (*A* and *B*) are blindfolded, or trusted to keep their eyes shut. A set of keys is placed in the circle by the teacher. *A*, the Keeper of the Keys, is then led into the circle, armed with a rolled up newspaper. *B*, the Thief, has to try to find the keys and get them out of the circle before being hit. If the Keeper hits the Thief s/he wins. If the Thief succeeds in removing the keys from the circle without being hit, s/he wins.

Simple variations include:

■ Neither *A* nor *B* knows the whereabouts of the keys.
■ If *B* is hit they are allowed to continue, but may not use that part of the body – i.e. if hit on arm, cannot use arm; if hit on head, dead!
■ *A* has keys tied loosely on a string to their foot – so that moving around the space reveals their whereabouts.
■ *A* sits on a chair with the keys beneath. In this version only *A* is blindfolded. *B* has to remove the keys within a given time limit.

Playing the game is not in itself drama, though a great deal of dramatic tension arises when it is well played. By treating the game as if it were a ritualised enactment of a story it is, however, possible to use it as a starting point for a drama, treating the players of the game as actors in a drama and the constraints, rules and conditions of the game as metaphors.

Each of the following questions is concerned with representation. If we are going to make up a play about The Keeper of the Keys:

■ I wonder who the Keeper is?
■ Who, or what, is trying to get the keys?
■ In the game, Keeper and Thief are both blindfolded; neither can see. Why? So what does the blindfold represent?
■ What does the circle represent?
■ What is the Keeper looking after? What do the keys represent?
■ What does the rolled-up newspaper represent?
■ And why does the Thief want to take the keys?

Different versions of the game will result in slightly different questions – but always focusing on issues of representation; the participants are taking on roles, the objects are simultaneously functioning as themselves and as metaphors. Here are two examples which evolved from questions like the above:

Class of Year 3 children

The Keeper is a guard who has been blinded to stop him ever setting eyes on a collection of magic jewels. He is armed with a silver sword, and spends most of his life in the dungeon beneath the castle where the jewels are kept, the circle of children in the game representing the walls of the dungeon. The 'thief' is the rightful owner of the jewels. Getting them back will enable her to free the prisoners in the castle.

Class of Year 6 children

Crew members take it in turns to guard the computer codes that enable their spaceship to take off. When anyone works as a guard they have to wear a blindfold because they are armed with a laser torch which is so powerful that it would blind them if they saw it. A clever alien wants to steal the spaceship, and knows about the laser torch, so puts on a blindfold as well. The computer codes are kept away from the spaceship in a cave with only one entrance (the circle of children watching the game played out).

Drama from story

In each of these examples we now have a story to which we do not know the end and a strong visual image, which we know has engaged the children. Although at this stage it is still a story and not yet a drama, that can lead us to an exciting starting point for a drama. If you tried to impose either of the above examples on another class I doubt the drama would work. In both of these, however, the children could see that they had created the story in collaboration with the teacher. They started the drama with ownership of the material.

Developing the game in this way is a lively and engaging way of opening up and exploring metaphorical language and meaning beyond the literal. Before moving on to the drama itself, it is worth giving further consideration to the symbolic potential of the images and objects. In both of these examples, the rolled-up newspaper represents a weapon which is simultaneously powerful and dangerous; using it creates risks. This is dramatically rich because it means that making a decision about using it is potentially difficult, in itself a dramatic situation. The teacher needs to be alert to the possibilities of exploring such symbolic meanings.

We now have a powerful image, a starting point for a drama which potentially offers rich learning opportunities; but we need to be sure that all the children in the class are going to be actively engaged. What roles are the children to play? If the teacher-in-role strategy is to be used, what role will the teacher play? What is likely to be an engaging and appropriate focus for our drama? What is the larger problem that we have to try to solve? It is sometimes helpful at this point to ask the children a further question:

> What might happen if the Thief (the rightful owner of the jewels/the alien in the above examples) does or does not manage to steal the 'keys'?

This might be termed the 'worst case syndrome'. Whatever answer the children provide also creates the fundamental dramatic tension behind the drama: if we don't manage to do X, then Y will occur. Although the drama might now start with replaying the game in this newly developed fictional context, the real drama begins when we start to explore the consequences of, for example, losing the computer codes from the alien and finding ourselves with no way of getting off the planet.

Note also that the children have seen that the outcome of the game cannot be pre-planned, and are likely to take this understanding with them to the drama itself.

Here are some ideas showing how one might develop a drama appropriate to the age range for each of the stories developed by children in the examples discussed above (pp. 181–2).

Prisoners in the Castle

- Children as villagers. Drama begins with teacher in role saying: 'I used to be a wizard with great powers; but my magic jewels have been stolen. Can you help me get them back? I know where they are; and I know there will be great risks involved in trying to get them back.' This drama might then focus initially on getting into the castle, might involve negotiating with other castle workers.

- Teacher as the guard, the children to decide upon their own role once the drama has started. Teacher: 'I cannot see, but I know you're there. What do you want? You can take the jewels if you want. They will do you no good.' In this case, the focus is likely to be on the dangers of having the magic jewels.

- The teacher says: 'Will somebody please help me get my brother out of prison?' This might lead to petitions to the King to release the prisoners in the castle.

Further questions which are likely to open up the Prisoners in the Castle drama

- What powers do the magic jewels have? (See 'Magic' in Chapter 4.)
- Why have the people been imprisoned?

- What sort of life does the guard lead? What sort of person is s/he?
- How could we talk to the guard?
- How can we be sure the jewels rightfully belong to the wizard?
- If we do get the jewels, what should we do with them?

The Stranded Spaceship

- Children as crew of spaceship, teacher as alien, going to the crew, asking for help: 'I admit that we've tried to steal your spaceship. That was wrong; but we desperately need to get off this planet. Will you help us?'
- Children as crew of spaceship, teacher as crew member, perhaps the guard on duty. Drama begins: 'I must have fallen asleep. The aliens have stolen the key; and now they've taken the spaceship. How are we going to survive on this planet?'
- Teacher as benevolent alien who cannot communicate with crew members (children), but wanted to learn their language.
- Children as aliens, teacher as crew member. Drama begins: 'We know you want to steal our spaceship. We'll let you travel in it if you will tell us all about yourselves, and show us your planet.'
- The reverse of the above, so that it is the children who are marooned on the alien planet, the teacher who is the alien offering them passage back to Earth providing the children can explain the way of life on Earth.

Further questions which are likely to open up the Stranded Spaceship *drama*

- What if the aliens are as frightened of us as we are of them?
- Why has the mission landed on this planet? What is the mission?
- How do the crew members feel about this planet?
- Why does the alien want to get into the spaceship?
- Could an alien have human feelings?
- How can we find out if the aliens mean us any harm?
- What benefits might there be from establishing a friendship with the aliens?
- What do the friends and relatives of the crew feel back on Earth as they await news?

The teacher might add the information that we need help from the aliens ourselves, or that the aliens look much more gentle than we had feared.

In a developing drama, the business of stealing the magic jewels or computer codes might soon become forgotten as the drama moves on to focus on the lives of those involved.

Developing scripts from this material

Although the above considers some possibilities for developing the game of Keeper of the Keys into drama, the game itself can be used in other ways – for example to teach about the nature of dramatic tension and dramatic structure.

Play the game normally, and then discuss why it's so exciting to watch. The reasons that are likely to emerge are:

- because we don't know what's going to happen;
- because the two participants come very close, but don't quite touch;
- because there are a number of near misses.

When children notice (as they usually do) that it is less enjoyable to watch when it's all over very quickly and there's not time for the tension to build up, you have a golden opportunity to relate this directly to narrative and dramatic structure. Resolving a situation and solving a problem too easily in drama makes it less interesting.

Now ask the children to play the game with their eyes open, but pretending they've got them shut. They have to make it as tense as they can. This is likely to stimulate active and fascinating discussion about the nature of drama, role play and structures of narrative.

Possible forms of a script

'Scripts' can take many different forms; the one we're most familiar with being the published playtext, with stage directions to suggest moves and lines of dialogue attributed to specific characters. But scripts can take other, simpler forms. Children's first attempts at creating scripts could take one of these forms:

- A storyboard is itself a form of script – as is a comic strip. Working with images is just as important as writing lines of dialogue. Seek clear visual paths through the 'play', using storyboards to show how the drama moves from one image to another.
- A summary of scenes, using words and pictures, indicating their running order, but not yet writing dialogue.

Developing a script with dialogue

- Having decided on which scenes are going to make up the whole play, use Forum Theatre (in small groups, or as a whole group) to develop a script for each scene, trying out different lines of dialogue and different ways of playing the scene (aggressive, frightened, hesitant, conciliatory, ready to compromise, defensive – in all sorts of different combinations) replaying it until it feels right, or has the effect that everybody is satisfied with.

- Within the developing drama, use the fiction to create opportunities for recording dialogue in role. For example, in *The Stranded Spaceship*, they need to record what is said between crew and alien, crew and Earth control.

- Record dialogue or message on video or audio and then transcribe and edit this. Again, the dramatic fiction can create a context for this: in *The Stranded Spaceship*, they might be running out of power and need to send an edited version of the dialogue with the alien back to Earth for analysis; or each crew member might have an opportunity to send a short message back to loved ones on Earth. They have to prepare what they want to say, make notes and then transmit. In each case the script has an interactive relationship with the developing drama.

11
Whale Island
Years 4–6

This example is based on workshops which were devised as part of a drama/poetry project for use with children in years 4 to 6 in schools from a variety of different catchment areas. In each case I began with the same starting point, although the drama rapidly diverged as the children took on the ideas and made the drama their own. When I taught the workshops in schools the sessions lasted about two hours. The material could, however, easily be adapted for use in the classroom and the school hall over a period of 3 to 4 weeks.

The example demonstrates how it is possible to use a narrative poem as a starting point for drama, and then use that drama in its turn as a stimulus for literacy work.

POSSIBLE NATIONAL CURRICULUM LINKS

Primary Framework for Literacy

Year 4 Poetry Unit 1

Speaking

- Respond appropriately to the contributions of others in light of differing viewpoints.

Drama

- Create roles showing how behaviour can be interpreted from different viewpoints.
- Develop scripts based on improvisation.

▶

Understanding and interpreting texts

- Explain how writers use figurative and expressive language to create images and atmosphere.

Engaging with and responding to texts

- Interrogate texts to deepen and clarify understanding and response.

Primary Framework for Literacy

Year 5 Poetry Unit 1

Drama

- Reflect on how working in role helps to explore complex issues.

Understanding and interpreting texts

- Infer writers' perspectives from what is written and from what is implied.

Engaging with and responding to texts

- Compare the usefulness of techniques such as visualisation, prediction and empathy in exploring the meaning of texts.

Primary Framework for Literacy

Year 6 Poetry Unit 1

Drama

- Improvise using a range of drama strategies and conventions to explore themes such as hopes, fears and desires.

Understanding and interpreting texts

- Understand underlying themes, causes and points of view.

Engaging with and responding to texts

- Sustain engagement with longer texts, using different techniques to make the text come alive.

PSHE & Citizenship KS2

Preparing to play an active role as citizens

- 2b   why and how rules and laws are made and enforced, why different rules are needed in different situations and how to take part in making and changing rules.

- 2e   to reflect on spiritual, moral, social, and cultural issues, using imagination to understand other people's experiences.

- 2f   to resolve differences by looking at alternatives, making decisions and explaining choices.

Developing good relationships and respecting the differences between people

- 4b   to think about the lives of people living in other places and times, and people with different values and customs.

The work uses the poem *Whale* by D.M. Thomas as the starting point for planning, although the children did not encounter the poem until after the workshops.

Whale

A whale lay cast up on the island's shore
in the shallow water of the outgoing tide.
He struggled to fill his lungs,
he grew acquainted with weight.

And the people came and said, Kill it, it is food.
And the witch-doctor said, It is sacred, it must not be harmed.
And a girl came and with an empty coconut-shell
scooped the seawater and let it run over the whale's blue bulk.

A small desperate eye showing white all round
the dark iris. The great head flattened against
sand as a face pressed against glass.

And a white man came and said, If all the people
  push we can float it off on the next tide.
And the witch-doctor said, It is taboo, it must not be touched.

And the people drifted away.
And the white man cursed and ran off to the next village for help.

And the girl stayed.
She stayed as the tide went out.
The whale's breath came in harsh spasms.
Its skin was darkening in the sun.
The girl got children to form a chain
of coconut-shells filled with fresh water
that she poured over his skin.

The whale's eye seemed calmer.

With the high tide the white man came back.
As the whale felt sea reach to his eye he reared
on fins and tail flukes, his spine arced
and he slapped it all down together, a great leap
into the same inert sand.
His eye rolled
in panic as again he lifted and crashed down,
  exhausted, and again lifted and crashed down,
    and again, and again.

The white man couldn't bear his agony and strode away
  as the tide receded.
He paced and paced the island and cursed God.

Now the whale didn't move.
The girl stroked his head
and as the moon came up
she sang to him
of friends long dead and children grown and gone,
sang like a mother to the whale,
and sang of unrequited love.

And later in the night
  when his breaths had almost lost touch
    she leant her shoulder against his cheek

and told him stories, with many details,
of the mud-skipping fish that lived
  in the mangroves on the lagoon.

Her voice
and its coaxing pauses was as if fins
were bearing him up to the surface of the ocean
to breathe and see,
as with a clot of blood falling on her brow
the whale passed clear from the body of his death.

D.M. Thomas

Planning considerations

The following is a simple narrative summary of the poem. A whale beaches itself on the shore. The islanders want to use it for food, but the 'witch doctor' says it must not be touched nor harmed. An outsider comes to the island people with what he considers to be superior knowledge. A girl responds to the whale and cares for it as best she can, daring to go against the authority of the 'witch doctor'. The poem explores the position that the girl finds herself in, caught between conflicting ideologies and yet finding strengths in herself as she comforts the whale.

Populating the drama

If we are to use this poem as a starting point for drama, we need first to consider the people involved. Whom does the poem refer to directly, and who might be implied by it? What are the possible roles for participants, and possible role(s) for the teacher? I list some of these as a brainstorming activity, a way of opening up possibilities.

People referred to directly in the poem:

- islanders with an elaborate set of taboos and sacred rituals;
- children of the island;
- a 'witch-doctor';
- a girl;
- a 'white man', an outsider to this community.

What other roles might be implied by the poem?

- the girl's friends and relatives;
- people who fish;
- a chief and elders from the island community;
- the boat crew that brought the 'white man' to the island;

- neighbouring islanders;
- tourists;
- a film crew.

At this point, having read the poem, thought about its dramatic content and possible roles, I need to decide:

- If I'm not going to ask the children simply to re-enact the narrative of the poem, what roles can they take on?
- Is there a role for the teacher in this drama? And if so, what will it be?
- What problem(s) are faced by the children in role, and what decisions can I ask them to make?

In the dramas I led using this poem, I have asked the children to play the islanders. I took on the role of the Chief of the tribe (not mentioned in the poem) and used that role to present the key problem: 'What shall we do about the whale?' In order to avoid pejorative associations, I referred to the 'Witch Doctor' of the poem as 'The Wise Woman'.

I decided that if I were to play the Chief, however, it would be better for that Chief to be weak. The reasoning behind this decision is discussed in detail in the section on *teaching in role* (Chapter 2). Put simply, it allows the teacher both to use the role to set up the drama and to hand over responsibility to the children for decision making at an early stage. If the Chief has all the power, the children's decision making is limited to 'Do we do as we're told, or not?!' – common enough in real life, but not very productive in drama.

In this instance, the Chief was going blind, unable to walk far, frightened of the Wise Woman and ready to give up power. The Chief referred to the Wise Woman, but she remained an offstage character in the drama, a lurking, slightly threatening absence.

The Whale Island drama

The poem itself was not read to the children until after the drama.

'Shut your eyes. Imagine . . . .' The island described by the teacher (out of role) as it would have appeared before the storm. The impression given is of a tropical paradise. 'I'll go away from the circle; when I come back I'll be playing a part in the drama. When I speak, open your eyes.'

Teacher returns in role. 'The gods are angry. In my long years the storm last night was the worst I have ever witnessed. I know that many of our dwellings are damaged beyond repair, fences have been blown down and I have heard that trees in the forest have been uprooted. Tell me what other damage there is. I cannot see it for myself. My eyes are weak, and I can no longer walk distances.'

The strategy of adopting the role of the leader who is losing his powers thus immediately enables the children to contribute actively; and to move into their own roles gently.

Time is given for children to respond to this. The teacher uses the role to draw meaning and significance from what they say; and then uses the role to inform and to raise the stakes in the drama.

'The Wise Woman came to me at first light. She said that now more than ever, we must keep to our customs. It was she who told me of the damage. She also said that she had walked to the centre of the island and from there – where it is possible to see the bay, the lagoon and the beaches – she could see many of your fishing boats smashed like crushed coconuts; but, worst of all, she told me that a whale lies cast up on the island's shore, in the shallow water of the outgoing tide; and that it is still alive. It is a warning from the gods.'

'We shall meet again here at the setting of the sun. Between now and then go about your business. Repair what you can. And go down to the shore. Look at the whale, but do not touch it. Act as my eyes, not my hands.'

The language is formal, almost ritualised, much of it drawn directly from the poem; but much is still left open to the children – e.g. the word 'dwellings' is used rather than the word 'huts', allowing the children to make decisions about the kinds of dwellings they have and to construct their own village.

With some out of role guidance from the teacher, the children play at repairing the village, rescuing animals and going down to the shore to see the whale.

The meeting at sunset

The teacher in role asks what they should do about the whale, again stressing that the Wise Woman has told him 'It is taboo . . . it must not be touched.' Out of role the teacher asks the children what they feel about the whale. About the Wise Woman? About the Chief? This is not a discussion. The children are asked to internalise their thoughts and feelings and then, briefly, to jot them down on a sheet of paper.

They then represent their feelings through still images. The teacher then comments (out of role) on their images, e.g. 'I can well understand your anger. I wonder when it will be sensible to express it?'

Teacher (out of role) – reflective narration: 'As the islanders went about their work the following day, they talked with others to find out what they wanted to do about the whale.' This gives the lead for discussion with the 'play' becoming more dramatic.

An opportunity to share these ideas at a meeting. The suggestions are discussed verbally or summarised through still image work, with the teacher interrogating each of the images, asking the class to do the same, and then enacting moments. The strategy of the weak Chief, with failing sight and unable to walk down to the shore, enables this sharing of images and enactments to be undertaken within the fiction of the drama. The Chief can say, 'Show all of us what you saw, but describe it for me.'

We also consider how they might represent the whale itself. Do we make a large class painting of the whale's head, or perhaps, using a roll of paper, a mural of the whale on the beach? Do we drape the gymnastics vaulting horse with cloth and pin a painting of the whale's eye to it? Do we chalk the outline of the whale's body (or head) on the floor of the hall?

To an audience which had not taken part in the making of this representation it could look simplistic or clumsy. But if the children have actively made the decision of how *to represent the whale and then made it themselves, it will considerably enhance their commitment to the drama.*

The ideas they expressed:

- keeping the whale wet;
- building a wall round it to make a pool and floating it off to sea;
- making medicine and taking it to the whale;
- disobeying the Chief and the Wise Woman and pushing the whale back out to sea.

That last suggestion is exciting and dangerous. It is these dangerous areas which are often the most productive dramatically. Drama has been described as taking place in a 'No Penalty Zone'. When we are taking part in a drama we can make mistakes, we can try out difficult decisions and see what happens; we don't have to impress our friends, we can afford not to be streetwise. We live with the consequences only for the duration of the drama. If the children choose to disobey the Chief, they have to deal with the consequences *in the drama*, where it is safe to take such dangerous decisions. In this instance, when children decided to disobey the Chief, I resigned: 'If you will not obey me, I can no longer be your Chief. I am too old and sick to command your respect.' This raised the stakes of the drama and shifted the focus. Although the immediate problem posed by the whale had been dealt with, the drama now focuses on power struggles within this non-technological community, about how the new Chief is to be chosen and about the relationship between the Chief (whoever it is to be) and the Wise Woman.

What to do when you have a number of conflicting suggestions? You can act on each of the suggestions in turn, or write down various different ideas on large sheets of paper or a whiteboard, according status to each. There are times when it is productive to turn the choice of what to do back to the children: 'Can we put both of those ideas together?' However, it's best not to get bogged down in lengthy discussions which will unnecessarily alienate the less articulate members of the class.

How to conclude?

The work described above could take place over several weeks. Chapter 5, 'Drama in an integrated curriculum', suggests ways of ensuring continuity and coherence when the work extends over a long period of time; but whether the drama lasts for an hour or for several weeks, we do eventually need to draw it to a close; and then we need to find ways of reflecting on the experiences of the drama – what has happened, what we've learned from it, what it might mean. One way is for the teacher to become a narrator, as described in Chapter 1.

With these workshops, all the sessions concluded with the children being asked to find a space on their own with writing and drawing materials. The teacher, out of role, asked a series of questions, to which they were asked to give an *individual* response:

'I'm going to ask a lot of questions. I don't expect you to answer all of them. Some of them may not interest you. You don't need to remember the questions. Start writing when you want to and use my questions as if they were your own thoughts. Write one word for your answer – or fill a page. Try to answer the questions in your head, and see if they make you ask more questions yourself.' The questions included:

- What colour is the whale?
- What does it feel like to touch?
- What does it smell of?
- What do you see in its eyes?
- What do you feel about it?
- How big is it compared with other things on the island?
- When you stand close to it, can you hear it making any sounds?

- If you could talk to the whale, and it could understand, what would you say?
- What does the whale dream of?
- What do you think the Chief feels about the whale?
- What do you think he feels about the Wise Woman?
- Why do you think the Wise Woman says it's wrong to touch the whale?
- Why do you think the Chief and the Wise Woman think that the gods are angry?
- What did you feel about the storm on the night when the whale came ashore?

Over the next few days the children were given opportunities to return to their writing and rework it until they were satisfied with it.

When they had completed their own written work the original poem was read to them – not as a model, but as an example of another response to a similar situation.

12
The Deserter
Years 4–6

A cross-curricular project, starting from and stimulating historical research, set in rural England during the English Revolution (1640–1660). Although the project, as documented here, was taught to children in Year 4 classes, the material is suitable for Years 4 to 6.

POSSIBLE NATIONAL CURRICULUM LINKS

The main focus of this drama was on moral and social issues, set in a historical context. Although it created numerous opportunities for developing literacy, I have focused on PSHE, Citizenship and History in the notes for this project.

PSHE & Citizenship KS2

'During key stage 2 PSHE and citizenship, children learn about themselves as growing and changing individuals with their own experiences and ideas, and as members of their communities.'

Developing confidence and responsibility and making the most of their abilities

- 1a   talking and writing about their opinions, and explaining their views, on issues that affect themselves and society.

- 1c   facing new challenges positively by collecting information, looking for help, making responsible choices, and taking action.   ▶

Preparing to play an active role as citizens

- 2e   reflecting on spiritual, moral, social and cultural issues, using imagination to understand other people's experiences.
- 2f   resolving differences by looking at alternatives, making decisions and explaining choices.

Developing good relationships and respecting the differences between people

- 4a   learning that their actions affect themselves and others, caring about other people's feelings and trying to see things from their points of view.
- 4b   thinking about the lives of people living in other places and times, and people with different values and customs.

History and historical enquiry

KS 2

The key here is the way that the drama stimulates research, and encourages enquiry. Although the drama itself is fictional, it provided a powerful stimulus to the children to find out about events of the period, how people lived and the changes in people's lives that took place at this time. In order to undertake this research they worked with a range of sources of information, including ICT-based sources, printed documents, CD-ROMS, databases, pictures and photographs. The drama also specifically gave them responsibility for asking important questions, and for selecting and recording information relevant to the focus of the enquiry.

Background

This example gives an account of a drama undertaken with two small classes of Year 4 children who worked together in the hall for the duration of this project – one whole afternoon, and the following morning. The example examines in detail some of the strategies and techniques used for exploring the consequences of a 'bad' decision. Two teachers were involved in this particular drama, but the underlying principles remain the same in all drama with any age group: find ways to slow the drama down and tease out the implications of decisions and actions. Although the children had little previous experience of drama and had not encountered the teacher-in-role strategy before, they had no difficulty with the teachers alternating between working in and out of role.

Preliminary work

The class takes on the role of a small rural community in mid-seventeenth-century England. After looking at various books and pictures of English rural life, they decide what jobs they will have in this community – woodcutting, farming, fishing, milling, etc. Teacher 1 enters in role as a parliamentarian official. Friendly but firm, he insists that they have to complete a census return, whilst at the same time acknowledging the appalling hardships they have had to endure during the recent Civil War. The *status* of the role is high, but not the highest – he is carrying out the orders of a higher authority; the *functions* of the role are to impart information (the sympathy expressed for the hardships is a way of communicating this to the children) and to set a challenge.

The census return has to include: who they are, where they live, what they do for a living. This simple listing task is tackled with great gusto, and deepens their commitment to their roles – the prime function of the task. When they have finished, they copy their work onto 'parchments' (sugar paper stained with weak tea!).

Raising the dramatic tension / questioning

Back in the drama, a stranger (Teacher 2, now in role) arrives in their village. He is injured and frightened and asks for their help. Out of role, Teacher 1 encourages the children to question the stranger. In small groups, the villagers prepare their questions for him – with the constraint that each group can only ask two questions. They give much thought and careful preparation to their questioning; the situation in the dramatic fiction providing a reason for the constraint – the stranger is too badly injured and too weak to be interrogated for long.

The subsequent questioning reveals that the stranger is a deserter from the army. Out of role, both teachers and the class discuss what it might mean to be a deserter at this time in history; and what some of the possible consequences might be if the deserter were to be found by those pursuing him. The discussion is gentle, while raising the stakes considerably. The class, excited by the danger of it, agree to hide him, providing he does his fair share of work.

One child asks, 'What if someone comes looking for him?' Teacher 1 (out of role) asks, 'Would you like to find out?' They do. Knowing that the parliamentarian official is likely to come back (although they don't know when he will return) with all the threats that creates for the village, substantially raises the dramatic tension.

With that tension lurking beneath the drama, each of the small working groups conspiratorially agrees on a task he is going to have to do for them – for example, the woodcutters want him to carry wood, the farmers for him to dig over some rough ground. Teacher 2 then assumes the role of the deserter again, and a small group go to him (watched by the rest of the class) to make the offer of sanctuary with its conditions: if he carries out a specific set of tasks every day, they are willing to give him shelter and food. The deserter says that he is very weak, and that he will do his best, but that he does not think he will be able to work as hard as they want him to. Using the technique of spotlighting, he moves from one group to another, and on each occasion cannot manage to fulfil the work required of him.

A bargain broken: what to do?

A meeting is convened by Teacher 1. What should they do? The deserter (deliberately positioned some way away from the meeting, as if out of earshot) has not fulfilled his part of the bargain. The class are split. The majority of children are keen to allow him food and shelter – the sophistication and humanity of the arguments for this are exhilarating: several children say that if they give him food and shelter he'll be able to build his strength back up, and then he'll be able to do the work. A minority, but still a fairly sizeable group argue that he should be sent away: 'The man from the army will be coming back.'

Then one boy says: 'I know what to do. I'll kill him.' This is a boy who has been on the periphery of things, not contributing actively until this moment; and many of the children in the class don't take the suggestion seriously. Teacher 2, however, seizes the moment and limps over to the meeting, in role as the deserter. There's a hush – the kind of dramatic hush that one only rarely hears in the professional theatre; one of those fascinating moments that is a response both in and out of role: in role, the villagers are shocked at the callousness of one of their number; out of role, the children are excited by what in other circumstances might be seen as a direct confrontational challenge to a teacher. The temptation is to use the power of the overwhelming majority to brush the suggestion aside. But that denies the extraordinary power of the moment – both dramatically and in terms of the learning opportunities it provides for the individual child and the class.

As the deserter, Teacher 2 addresses the whole class with solemn formality: 'He's right. I have to contribute. I cannot ask you to shelter me, provide sanctuary for me, when to do so puts all of you in danger. My injuries are too serious and I am too weak to survive.' And then turning to the boy who made the suggestion: 'How do you know about killing?'

'I'm a soldier.'

'You're a skilled and experienced soldier?'

'Yes.'

'And you would know how to kill me quickly and painlessly?'

'Yes.'

'If I am to die, I would far rather die quickly at the hands of a skilled man, surrounded by good people, than wander off into the forest and die like a wounded animal; or, worse, be tortured by those in the army who want to punish me.'

The boy, whose suggestion may well have been glib, has been taken very seriously. In the fictions that these children are familiar with, killing is often trivialised; an easy solution, often glamorous and almost always inconsequential. Here it is made weighty and highly significant. He and the village will have to 'live' with the consequences of whatever decision is made.

Conscience alley

Teacher 1, out of role, stops the meeting; and asks the children to shut their eyes and reflect on what has happened, and what might be about to happen. He asks the children to form two lines in parallel, and the deserter to walk slowly through the 'alley'. As he passes each child, they can say what they think the deserter might be feeling. This ranges from 'Sad' and 'Lonely' through 'He wishes he hadn't come to this village' to 'He wants the pain to go away' and 'He wants to be brave, but he hopes somebody stops the soldier from killing him.'

Teacher 1 then asks him to walk slowly back in the other direction; and again the children speak as he passes them. But this time they say what each of them, as a villager, thinks about the deserter.

Then he asks the boy who has constructed the role of the soldier for himself to do the same, to stand at the end of the two lines and walk slowly through the 'alley', while the other children in the class speak what they imagine he might be thinking as he prepares to take the life of the deserter.

In other circumstances, it might have been appropriate to allow the villagers an opportunity to tell the soldier what they think about him; but here, the boy was clearly as nervous as he was thrilled to be the centre of such attention and a judgement was made that to pursue this might break the protection that the role had hitherto provided for him. At the end of this sequence of activities, Teacher 2, the deserter, asks to speak with the soldier alone. The rest of the class gather round in a semi-circle to watch the subsequent exchange in Forum style.

The deserter says, 'I admire your skill and your courage. You are obviously confident with a sword. I was always frightened in battle. But before you take my life, allow me to thank those who have looked after me.'

At this point, an extraordinary thing happens: the boy, who has hitherto been virtually silent since making his intervention about killing, says, 'I cannot kill you. There are people in the village who can help you. They have ointments and things. They'll make you better.'

'Are you playing with me soldier?' asks the deserter. The boy shakes his head and, in mime, he lays down his 'sword'.

An alternative ending – enacting the killing

In this drama, the boy refused to undertake the killing. But had he been willing to go ahead, that, too could have been dramatised. The deserter might have asked him to describe exactly what he intended to do, to prepare him so that the killing was as painless as possible; and for him to enact it in very slow motion. It would, however, also be important to involve the whole of the class in this as actively as possible. There is a technique, adapted from one used by Brecht in rehearsals, for dealing with moments of high action and emotion: the teacher asks the children one by one to speak aloud in the third person whatever each does, thinks and feels as they do it. In this instance, for example, one of the children might say, 'The woodcutter is feeling angry, and he gets up and walks away.' Another might say, 'The woman who knows about herbs is upset because she thinks she could have helped him back to health. She cries and looks down at the ground.'

The return of the census officer

In the drama which actually took place, however, the villagers decide to care for the deserter; those in the village with a knowledge of herbs and medicines nursing him (resulting in a wealth of cross-curricular work in the ensuing weeks) until he's fit to work properly. Teacher 1 returns as the parliamentarian official, to collect the census returns. They admit they have a visitor. The class plead for mercy on his behalf. The official asks to see the deserter, recognises him, and agrees that he is too badly injured to travel and too weak to pose a threat. He says he would like to spare him, but it is not his decision; the Lord Protector makes these decisions. The drama concludes with the villagers writing letters to Cromwell, The Lord Protector, pleading for mercy. These were written with an extraordinary formality, but the content was deeply moving. In order to save the deserter's life the letters had to be good.

13
The Coming of the Railway
Years 5–6

This example began life as a historical project, focusing on Victorian Britain. It involved work in most curriculum areas. For clarity – and in order to draw attention to the interrelationships between the work in drama and in other curriculum areas – I have divided the account of this project into 'Drama time' and 'Class time'. In reality the divisions were not so distinct, and 'Class time' included ICT research, work in the school library, homework, work on the school field and visiting a local museum.

Aims

- to explore the impact that changes in work and transport might have had on the lives of men, women and children from different sections of society;

- to examine the effect that railway building might have had on a rural community;

- to explore the conflicts of loyalty that might arise between people when faced with major changes in their way of life;

- to explore the ways in which developments in science and new technology affect the circumstances of human life and culture.

POSSIBLE NATIONAL CURRICULUM LINKS

This drama is set in a historical context. Although it created numerous opportunities for developing and enhancing literacy, I have focused on History, PSHE and Citizenship in the notes for this project.

History KS2

The project was based on the National Curriculum Victorian Britain 'study of the impact of significant individuals, events and changes in work and transport on the lives of men, women and children from different parts of society.'

Knowledge and understanding of events, people and changes in the past

3 Pupils should be taught:

- a) about characteristic features of the periods and societies studied, including the ideas, beliefs, attitudes and experiences of men, women and children in the past.

- c) to identify and describe reasons for, and results of, historical events, situations, and changes in the periods studied.

Historical enquiry

4 Pupils should be taught:

- a) how to find out about the events, people and changes studied from an appropriate range of sources of information, including ICT-based sources.

- b) to ask and answer questions, and to select and record information relevant to the focus of the enquiry.

Organisation and communication

5 Pupils should be taught to:

- a) recall, select and organise historical information.

- c) communicate their knowledge and understanding of history in a variety of ways.

▶

> ## PSHE & Citizenship KS2
>
> **Preparing to play an active role as citizens**
>
> *2 Pupils should be taught:*
>
> - a) to research, discuss and debate topical issues, problems and events.
> - e) to reflect on spiritual, moral, social, and cultural issues, using imagination to understand other people's experiences.
> - f) to resolve differences by looking at alternatives, making decisions and explaining choices.
>
> **Developing good relationships and respecting the differences between people**
>
> *4 Pupils should be taught:*
>
> - a) that their actions affect themselves and others, to care about other people's feelings and to try to see things from their points of view.
> - b) to think about the lives of people living in other places and times, and people with different values and customs.

The drama project

Class time

Preliminary work, undertaken before the children embark on the drama, involves research into nineteenth-century life, including looking at maps of the local area prior to the coming of the railway. Working in small groups, children research one item invented since 1850. 'What do we use in our lives now which people didn't have a hundred years ago?' Examples: refrigerator, electric light, motor car, biro, telephone.

Drama time

Preparatory 'Twilight' activities (see p. 62)

Mime work in pairs:

A mimes a simple activity, using gadget(s) from today; *B* has to achieve the same end result by using materials available in the early nineteenth century, e.g.

- *A* makes breakfast using fridge and electric cooker;
- *B* milks cow, draws water from well, chops firewood, lights fire, takes eggs from chicken, etc.!

The community

A small imaginary town is established, and a name agreed for it – Seatown. Children agree on roles within small groups (farmers, miners, shopkeepers, mill workers, etc.), then create still images of these people at work. Teacher comments.

The commitment to the roles is strengthened through improvisation work in small groups. Each group has to solve a minor problem (e.g. broken fence, rats in the flour, not enough wood for the fire) then interact with other groups by trading in the market place. The teacher takes on a role as a member of the local council who has been away on business. He returns with the news that he has been asked to ensure that the Parish Registries are all up to date. In the meantime he has to go back to the nearby town on further business – but first his horse needs shoeing, his cart needs repairing and he needs food and shelter. He talks about how difficult the journey is these days with the roads in such a bad state, and how more trade would come to the town if the transportation links were better.

The role chosen by the teacher here is as neutral as possible. The role does, however, have several functions: seeking shelter and help with shoeing his horse and repairing his cart are ways of intervening in small group work, using the role to value and focus it ('I am so glad I can rely on people here to do a good job'); talking about transport difficulties conveys contextual information which will become important at a later stage in the drama; and asking the children to update the Parish Registries is a way of not only making their role play more concrete but also stimulating historical enquiry.

Class time

The children examine original documents loaned from the local library, showing what a parish registry from this period would have looked like. They then create their own 'Parish Registry' – a way of confirming and deepening their commitment to the roles they've adopted. Further research into rural lifestyles in the 1850s.

Drama time

The teacher returns in role to collect the new Registry – and comment on its usefulness. He also enthuses about the extraordinary steam trains he has recently seen for himself, reading from a journal which he has been writing while away. This description is taken from a contemporary source. Wherever possible, it is good to use authentic contemporary material. Children are excited by it; it helps reinforce the children's understanding of and commitment to the time shift, and in this case introduces the idea of a journal as part of the fiction, thereby leading into other writing-in-role activities.

Surveying

The teacher also brings a large, but incomplete, map of the town and surrounding area, saying that he's been approached by one of the railway companies who are interested in building a railway line to Seatown, and that they have asked him to have the map updated. The map shows the town is close to the sea, has a natural harbour, but is cut off from nearby large towns by hills and a large marsh.

Class time

The children work in small groups to complete the map provided. Map work is organised in such a way that children of all levels of ability can contribute and ranges from pictorial mapping (placing a picture of a windmill on the map) to working with simple map symbols, contour lines and co-ordinates. As a complementary activity, children use the school field to undertake some elementary surveying.

A growing body of material is provided to create opportunities for possible research – recommended websites are complemented by books, photographs, documentation, letters describing reactions to the railway, facsimiles of original maps, old newspapers and prints.

Drama time

After recapping and reflecting on the work undertaken so far by asking small groups to create a sequence of still images, the teacher explains that he will now be taking on a different role. A meeting is held which he attends in role as a railway contractor. He is carrying the map the class have made, which his 'friend' has delivered; he thanks them for the excellent job they have done.

'I am a contractor, not a surveyor. Surveying is clearly something that many of you are very good at. We want to build a line which will connect Seatown with the big industrial cities. And we need your help with the survey.'

As the meeting progresses, it becomes clear that the railway link will be expensive, involving tunnelling through the hills and building a viaduct across the marsh. In order to cut costs elsewhere the company want to build the line right through the middle of the town and across much of the farmland which the children have established (in role) as belonging to them. Some children want the railway and are prepared to help with the survey, while others want things to remain as they are, and this group want to organise resistance to the coming of the railway.

There are potential organisational problems in allowing the group to split into two such distinct factions. There is not only a danger of the drama becoming confrontational, but the focus can split, resulting in confusion and loss of control. This is less of a problem if *team-teaching* is a possibility. If you're working alone, one way of dealing with it is for the class to look at each side in turn: they can all play the townspeople who want to join the survey team, and then all play those who don't want the railway to come through the town. The potential for confrontation does, however, create opportunities for practising and developing skills of negotiating, persuading, listening, and compromising. Another way of dealing with it would be to use some of the methods of Forum Theatre (see Chapter 2). You, the teacher, might take on one role, with the class advising the person who is negotiating with you.

Class time

Discussion and research about railway lines, need for straightness and low gradients. Historical research into survey methods. Discussion about industrialisation and possible effects of *not* letting the railway be built. We do not yet, however, discuss what *might* happen in our drama.

Drama time

The children start by working in small groups, continuing to improvise their daily routine, but with the added task that while they are working they should discuss the issue of the railway route. Out of role, the teacher moves from group to group, occasionally spotlighting one of them, saying 'Let's see what's happening in different parts of the town' and then reflecting, valuing and high-lighting the significance of what has been heard and seen. Small groups asked to create still images of the conflicting feelings. A short scene played out (using Forum Theatre) between farmers and the railway engineer (teacher in role), who tries to persuade them to sell their land to the railway company. The teacher uses this opportunity to introduce the idea that the railway will open up new markets. When I first led this drama with children, they were persuaded to accept the railway at this point, and the drama appeared to be over! They were too easily persuaded to sell their land and houses. This might well have happened in 'real life' on occasions, but if we are using drama to teach children about the impact of transport changes on the lives of people it will need to open up and explore the *dilemmas* of industrialisation. In this case it seems that the structure of the drama made it too easy for the children – perhaps because of the non-confrontational role adopted by the teacher as messenger early on, when he was excited and enthusiastic about the railway and its effect on another town.

This particular session ends with the railway engineer offering contracts of employment to those townspeople who want to work for the railway on the construction of the line.

Raising the stakes

That is not the end of the drama. One of the advantages of using drama in this way (with the narrative continuing over several weeks) is that both the teacher and the children can change roles, enabling you to look at any given topic from different points of view.

Class time

The map is marked up with the Lots that have been sold. Research begins on the materials needed for railway construction, with some children producing a newspaper (on computer) reporting what has been happening in the town – which they 'sell' in the next drama session. Others write letters (in role) to relatives and friends in other parts of the country telling them what has happened, and (for the most part) excitedly proclaiming how easy it will be to visit once the line is built. Work also begins on planning the construction of a bridge. How will the line cross the marshes? Model making, drawing, scientific testing of materials and further historical research.

Drama time

The teacher relates the 'story' of the drama so far, taking care to include reference to all the groups of children – but concluding:

> So the railway engineer's job appeared to be complete. He was about to go back to the company when he realised that in the middle of the town was a house where an old man lived, exactly where the company were planning to build their new station. The old man was refusing to sell.

The teacher asks the children what they know about the old man. Together they 'construct' the role, which the teacher then takes on. Using the techniques of forum theatre, the class try to persuade the old man to sell his house and land.

A letter arrives from the railway company, stating that if they cannot purchase all the necessary land for the agreed route, they'll pull out.

Class time

Research task: looking at maps of Britain in 1840, 1890 and today. Did any towns thrive which were *not* connected to the railway system?

Drama time

The pressure is on. How will they persuade the old man to leave his house? Should they? There's no easy moralising here. It's tough and difficult. Through their research the class know that not being connected to the railway will mean rapid decline. Many of the townspeople want to threaten the old man with violence. It's tempting to stop the drama at such morally dubious moments – but (as in 'The Deserter', above) it is precisely here that the greatest learning opportunities are offered. If we are to examine the consequences of actions, we must allow 'bad' choices, whilst using the protection of role to ensure that children see this as fiction. In this instance, the teacher's decision to take on the role of the old man allows a formal device to deal with the threats:

> Collaboratively, we create an image of the interior of the house where the old man lives; careful questioning building up a shared image based on photographs and sketches they have seen of authentic nineteenth-century housing.

> From the generalised sense of the house, we move on to focusing on the person inside it. The teacher sits on a chair in the centre of a circle and, out

of role, asks the children to shut their eyes and imagine: 'What do you think he is feeling?' 'What does he remember about this house?'

When the image has become more concrete, and the children's perceptions of the old man have moved from thinking of him as an irritation, an inconvenient obstacle, to a person with memories and strong reasons for wanting to stay where he is, they are asked to approach him one at a time and tell him what they want him to do. If they still want to threaten him, they can do so. The overall tone changes and most children attempt to persuade, though some still make unpleasant threats, including: 'If you don't move out, we'll burn your house down.'

When all who want to have had their say, the teacher comes out of role and asks everybody to close their eyes again; and each to imagine themselves as the old man. 'I wonder what he's feeling now?' They open their eyes and, using the technique of *spotlighting*, the teacher asks them to speak their thoughts aloud.

Their expressions of the old man's feelings are insightful and moving; an indication of the extent to which it is possible for children to move between roles, once they have built their commitment to the drama. After the threats and the attempts at persuasion, the old man reluctantly agrees to leave his house. The railway will come through. The bullies appear to have triumphed. But then the class are divided into small groups and asked to make two still images showing what the townspeople might be feeling at this moment – first about their success in getting the railway to the town, and second about what they have done to the old man, who is now homeless.

Each member of the class is asked to think quietly: 'Listen to your own thoughts for a moment or two . . .' then 'If there is something you want to say to him, go to him and say it now.' The project finishes there, with the children expressing considerable remorse for getting the old man out of his home, but they have learned far more about morality this way than they would have done if they had been stopped from making their threats.

Although this project was not taken any further, it is not necessarily 'the end'. What happens to the old man? What happens during the construction of the railway? What happens to people ten years later who leave their small town and go to the big city to find work? We could easily move on to a project exploring other aspects of Victorian England.

There is a key 'branching' decision being made in the drama described above – when the children decide to accept the coming of the railway, or turn it away. The drama comes not from discussing what each decision *might* mean, but in making the decision and working through the consequences.

In a drama based on a similar starting point another group of children vehemently refused to let the engineer carry out the survey – and the focus of the drama shifted: how do people cope with rural decline, losing markets and jobs? In this instance they decided to emigrate! The drama continues – reaching out, as ever, into exciting areas of exploration in history, geography and science.

5

Resources

Here you will find a list of recommended books and journals, together with a brief appraisal of each; suggestions for associated film, television and DVD material, online resources and Internet links; the bibliography and the index.

Content

14
Resources

Recommended books and journals

Full bibliographic information appears in the bibliography below.

Baldwin, P. (2004) *With Drama in Mind: Real Learning in Imagined Worlds*

For drama specialists and non-specialists alike. Offers a rationale for teaching through drama and introduces a range of drama strategies and units of work. Includes a range of photocopiable materials for use in the classroom.

Baldwin and Fleming (2003) *Teaching Literacy Through Drama*

'Designed to help teachers meet National Curriculum and National Literacy Strategy requirements through the integration of speaking, listening, reading and writing.' More focused on speaking and listening than on writing.

Boal, Augusto (1979) *Theatre of the Oppressed*

This is the book where Boal first proposed his ideas for Forum Theatre. The book places this in a theatrical context, relating it to the theories of Aristotle and Brecht.

Boal, Augusto (1992) *Games for Actors and Non-Actors*

The book contains further work on Forum Theatre. Although there is some theoretical underpinning, this is more of a handbook of ideas and exercises than *Theatre of the Oppressed*. There is much in here about Image Theatre.

Egan, Kieran (2006) *Teaching Literacy: Engaging the Imagination of New Readers*

A wise and witty book which integrates accessible theory with numerous engaging practical examples that focus on teaching literacy through story, 'using concepts ranging from fascinating to exotic to magnificent to weird'. Egan's aim is to foster a 'lifelong love of reading and writing'. Although it is not directly about drama, this is an inspirational book; and the pedagogical principles proposed are entirely appropriate for drama teaching.

Fines, John and Verrier, Ray (1974) *The Drama of History*

This is now sadly out of print, but it remains an excellent book. It's delightfully entertaining and as useful to the non-specialist as to the specialist. It's specifically about using drama to teach history, but it contains a wealth of wisdom about teaching drama (and indeed teaching itself). Chapter 8 (pp. 79–91) includes an entertaining and intelligent discussion of the issue of finding the balance between the need for authenticity while not intimidating children. One of the best books written on cross-curricular learning.

Heathcote, D. and Bolton, G. (1995) *Drama for Learning: Dorothy Heathcote's Mantle of the Expert Approach to Education*

A collection of illuminating essays by Dorothy Heathcote and Gavin Bolton, edited by Cecily O'Neill.

Morgan, N. and Saxton, J. (1987) *Teaching Drama*

Although this is currently out of print, it is an excellent book, which is useful for primary and secondary alike. Full of good sound practical advice, usefully combined with good theory to give a strong sense of direction. Particularly useful are the chapters on Teacher in role, Questioning and Answering, and Planning.

O'Neill, C. (1995) *Drama Worlds: A framework for process drama*

A detailed and important examination of process drama, considering its relationships with other kinds of dramatic improvisation. Focuses on the texts that process drama generates, the kinds of roles available, factors such as audience and dramatic time, and the leader's function in the event. She provides examples of several process dramas and identifies key dramatic strategies and characteristics.

Taylor, P. and Warner, C. (eds) (2006) *Structure and Spontaneity: the process drama of Cecily O'Neill*

A compilation of Cecily O'Neill's formative writings about process drama, together with significant commentaries.

Toye, N. and Prenderville, F. (2000) *Drama and traditional story for the early years*

One of the best books about drama with children in early years. It contains such a wealth of excellent material, and the methodology is so sound and clearly set out, that it would also be useful to anyone working with all children in lower primary. Contains 16 full dramas and more than 30 starting points for development.

Wagner, B.-J. (1979) *Dorothy Heathcote: Drama As a Learning Medium*

The first book to discuss Dorothy Heathcote's innovative methods and pedagogy. A great deal of excellent practice described in this book. Particularly useful for its chapters on planning and working in role. Now republished in a revised edition by Trentham Books.

Winston, J. (2004) *Drama and English at the Heart of the Primary Curriculum*

A practical handbook which considers what is meant by 'good' drama; in Joe Winston's words, 'drama that includes but goes beyond closely defined learning objectives'. Contains suggestions for activities, guidance on teaching techniques, step-by-step guides, lesson plans and analysis; examples of cross-curricular drama work including whole school approaches.

Playwriting and creative writing

Greig, Noel (2004) *Playwriting: A Practical Guide*

Noel Greig has run numerous workshops on playwriting 'in a wide range of communities and contexts', including primary and secondary schools. The book contains well over a hundred different exercises, all of which can be adapted. An excellent book, thoroughly recommended.

Hughes, Ted (1967) *Poetry in the Making*

First published in 1967, this is still an inspirational book. Based on a series of programmes that Hughes wrote for BBC Schools, it was intended for use as a text and an anthology for use in class or as a handbook for teachers and writers. Although the book makes no references to plays as such, it contains excellent advice – especially about the importance of close observation and attention to detail. There is much material here that could be used with children in upper primary.

Woolland, B. (2008) *Pupils as Playwrights: drama, literacy and playwriting*

There are several books about playwriting for adults and students in secondary, but, to my knowledge, this is the only book that is specifically aimed at the primary school age range. It includes extensive practical exercises, activities and case studies of developed process drama. It makes explicit links between drama, literacy and the development of speaking and listening skills, including photocopiable material which can be used with children, together with advice on how to develop similar materials.

Journals

The Journal for Drama in Education

Contains an invigorating and stimulating mix of articles (both practical and theoretical) about all aspects of teaching drama with all ages and abilities. Published twice yearly by the National Association for the Teaching of Drama. Web address below.

Teaching, Thinking & Creativity Magazine

'Dedicated to promoting critical and creative thinking at both primary and secondary level.' Is not focused on drama, and only occasionally published articles specifically about drama; but does contain useful material. Published 4 times a year. Imaginative Minds, The Custard Factory, 215 The Green House, Gibb Street, Birmingham, B9 4AA, UK.

Film, television and DVD material

The British Film Institute has developed an excellent teaching guide to using film and television with 3 to 11-year-olds, entitled *Look Again!* It outlines the close connections between teaching literacy and cineliteracy, and shows how to integrate these activities across the curriculum in primary schools. The BFI also produce *Starting Stories* for primary schools. Further information on BFI website below.

Film Education offers a wealth of free educational materials, resources and services which have been developed in response to the growing importance of Media Education in the National Curriculum.

Film: 21st Century Literacy aims to 'help children and young people to use, enjoy and understand moving images; not just to be technically capable but to be culturally literate too . . .'.

Online resources and Internet links

Drama in education

Bealings School Mantle of the Expert projects
http://www.bealings.org.uk/exciting-projects/mantle-of-the-expert/

Dorothy Heathcote Archive
http://www.partnership.mmu.ac.uk/dha/

Initial Teacher Education, Drama at Key Stages 1 and 2
This site is a collaboration between the National Association for the Teaching of English and the United Kingdom Literacy Association.
http://www.ite.org.uk/ite_topics/drama_at_KS1-2/013.html

London Drama
http://www.londondrama.org/

Mantle of the Expert
http://www.mantleoftheexpert.com/index.php

NATD, the National Association for the Teaching of Drama
http://www.natd.net/

National Drama
http://www.nationaldrama.co.uk/

Film

British Film Institute resources for Primary Schools
http://www.bfi.org.uk/education/teaching/primary.html

Film Education
http://www.filmeducation.org/

Film: 21st Century Literacy
http://21stcenturyliteracy.org.uk/

National Curriculum and Educational Reports

Cambridge Primary Review
http://www.primaryreview.org.uk/

Drama in schools (Arts Council England document)
http://www.artscouncil.org.uk/documents/publications/725.pdf

National Curriculum Creativity documentation
http://curriculum.qca.org.uk/key-stages-1-and-2/learning-across-the-curriculum/creativity/index.aspx

Primary Framework for literacy and mathematics – literacy learning objectives
http://www.standards.dcsf.gov.uk/primaryframework/literacy/lo_new

Theatre and Theatre in Education

Applied & Interactive Theatre Guide
http://www.tonisant.com/aitg/

Big Brum Theatre in Education Company
http://www.bigbrum.org.uk/

National Theatre website. The National Theatre has an active Education Department. Their *Primary Shakespeare Project* focuses on literacy, oracy, creative writing, drama, music, design and movement for Year 5 and Year 6 classes and their teachers.
http://www.nationaltheatre.org.uk/education

University of Exeter has a webpage which gives links to most UK Theatre in Education companies:
http://spa.ex.ac.uk/drama/links/theatreedu.html

Bibliography

Agard, J. (1991) in *Can I buy a Slice of the Sky*, Nichols, Grace (ed.), London: Blackie and Sons Ltd.

Alexander, R.J. (2009) *Towards a New Primary Curriculum: a report from the Cambridge Primary Review. Part 2: The Future*, Cambridge: University of Cambridge Faculty of Education.

Arts Council of England (2003) *Drama in Schools*, 2nd edition, London: Arts Council England.

Baldwin, P. (2004) *With Drama in Mind: Real Learning in Imagined Worlds*, Stafford: Network Educational Press.

Baldwin, P. and Fleming, K. (2003) *Teaching Literacy Through Drama: Creative Approaches*, London: Routledge Falmer.

Boal, A. (1979) *Theatre of the Oppressed*, London: Pluto.

Boal, A. (1992) *Games for Actors and Non-Actors*, London: Routledge.

Bolton, G. (1984) *Drama as Education*, Longman.

Bolton, G. (1998) *Acting in Classroom Drama: a critical analysis*, Stoke on Trent: Trentham.

Bond, E. (1999) *The Hidden Plot: Notes on Theatre and the State*, London: Methuen.

Bowell, P. and Heap, B. (2001) *Planning Process Drama*, London: David Fulton.

Brecht, B. (1964) (trans. Willett, J.) *Brecht on Theatre*, London: Methuen.

Browne, A. (1989) *The Tunnel*, London: Julia MacRae Books.

Courtney, R. (1968) *Play Drama and Thought*, London: Cassell.

Davis, D. (ed.) (2005) *Edward Bond and the Dramatic Child*, Stoke on Trent: Trentham.

Egan, K. (2006) *Teaching Literacy: Engaging the Imagination of New Readers*, London: Sage Publications.

Fines, J. and Verrier, R. (1974) *The Drama of History*, London: New University Education.

Freire, P. (1970) *Pedagogy of the Oppressed*, London: Penguin Books.

Gardner, H. (1999) *Intelligence Reframed: multiple intelligences for the 21st century*, New York: Basic Books.

Greig, N. (2005) *Playwriting*, London: Routledge.

Heathcote, D. and Bolton, G. (1995) *Drama for Learning: Dorothy Heathcote's Mantle of the Expert Approach to Education*, London: Heinemann.

Hughes, T. (1967) *Poetry in the Making*, London: Faber and Faber.

Hughes, T. (1968) *The Iron Man: A Story in Five Nights*, London: Faber and Faber.

Johnson L. and O'Neill C. (eds) (1984) *Dorothy Heathcote – Collected writings on education and drama*, London: Hutchinson.

McKee, D. (1980) *Not Now Bernard*, London: Andersen Press.

Morgan, N. and Saxton, J. (1987) *Teaching Drama*, London: Hutchinson.

National Advisory Committee on Creative and Cultural Education (1999) *All Our Futures: Creativity, culture and education*, London: DfEE.

O'Neill, C. (1995) *Drama Worlds: A framework for process drama*, London: Heinemann.

O'Neill, C. and Lambert, A. (1982) *Drama Structures: A practical handbook for teachers*, Cheltenham: Stanley Thornes.

Roethke, Theodore (1975) *The Collected Poems of Theodore Roethke*, New York: Anchor Books.

Tan, S. (2006) *The Arrival*, New York: Arthur A. Levine Books.

Taylor, P. and Warner, C. (eds) (2006) *Structure and Spontaneity: the process drama of Cecily O'Neill*, Stoke on Trent: Trentham.

Thomas, D.M. (1983) *Selected Poems*, London: Secker and Warburg.

Toye, N. and Prenderville, F. (2000) *Drama and traditional story for the early years*, London and New York: Routledge Falmer.

Toye, N. and Prenderville, F. (2007) *Speaking and Listening Through Drama 7–11*, London: Paul Chapman Publishing.

Vygotsky, L. (1978) *Mind in Society: Development of Higher Psychological Processes*, Cambridge, MA: Harvard University Press.

Wagner, B.-J. (1979) *Dorothy Heathcote: Drama As a Learning Medium*, London: Hutchinson.

Winston, J. (2000) *Drama, Literacy and Moral Education 5–11*, London: David Fulton.

Winston, J. (2004) *Drama and English at the Heart of the Primary Curriculum*, London: David Fulton.

Woodhouse, J. (2001) *The Life & Work of Pieter Bruegel*, Oxford: Heinemann.

Woolland, B. (2008) *Pupils as Playwrights: drama, literacy and playwriting*, Stoke on Trent: Trentham.

Woolland, B. (2009) 'What did you make of that?', in *The Journal for Drama in Education*, Vol. 26, Issue 1, Spring 2009, NATD.

Index